Will Big Business Destroy Our Planet?

Peter Dauvergne

Will Big Business Destroy Our Planet?

polity

The right of Peter Dauvergne to be identified as Author of this Work has been asserted in accordance with the UK Copyright, Designs and Patents Act 1988.

First published in 2018 by Polity Press

Reprinted 2018

Polity Press
65 Bridge Street
Cambridge CB2 1UR, UK

Polity Press
101 Station Landing
Suite 300
Medford, MA 02155, USA

ISBN-13: 978-1-5095-2400-6 (hardback)
ISBN-13: 978-1-5095-2401-3 (paperback)

A catalogue record for this book is available from the British Library.

Library of Congress Cataloging-in-Publication Data
Names: Dauvergne, Peter, author.
Title: Will big business destroy our planet? / Peter Dauvergne.
Description: Cambridge, UK ; Medford, MA : Polity Press, [2018] | Series:
    Environmental futures | Includes bibliographical references and index.
Identifiers: LCCN 2017042180 (print) | LCCN 2017050832 (ebook) | ISBN
    9781509524044 (Epub) | ISBN 9781509524006 (hardback) | ISBN 9781509524013
    (pbk.)
Subjects: LCSH: Big business--Environmental aspects. | Sustainable
    development. | Social responsibility of business.
Classification: LCC HC79.E5 (ebook) | LCC HC79.E5 D34634 2018 (print) | DDC
    363.7/011--dc23
LC record available at https://lccn.loc.gov/2017042180

Typeset in 11 on 15 pt Sabon by
Servis Filmsetting Ltd, Stockport, Cheshire
Printed and bound in the UK by CPI Group (UK) Ltd, Croydon CR0 4YY

For further information on Polity, visit our website: politybooks.com

Contents

Acknowledgments

I am grateful to Louise Knight at Polity Press for inspiring this book, Nekane Tanaka Galdos at Polity Press for editorial assistance, and to Michaela Pedersen-Macnab for her adept research support. I am also thankful for the perceptive feedback from Polity's anonymous reviewers for this book. Jane Lister, my coauthor for the books *Timber* (2011) and *Eco-Business* (2013), and Genevieve LeBaron, my coauthor for the book *Protest Inc.* (2014), deserve special mention here, as their insights into the environmental and social consequences of big business have greatly influenced my thinking over the past decade.

A grant from the Social Sciences and Humanities Research Council of Canada supported the research for this book (Corporations and the Politics of Environmental Activism in the Global South, reference number 435–2014–0115).

1

Total Destruction?

The earth is in crisis. And this crisis is escalating. The planet is growing warmer and warmer, bringing increasingly violent storms, prolonged droughts, rising seas, scorching forest fires, and the extinction of species. And this is far from our only worry. Coral reefs are dying. Fish stocks are collapsing. Industrial pollutants are poisoning the Arctic. And toxic chemicals are leaching into aquifers.

Signs of an escalating global environmental crisis are everywhere. Swirling eddies of plastic are growing ever-larger in the Pacific, Atlantic, and Indian oceans, with the largest, known as the "Great Pacific Garbage Patch," bigger than the state of Texas. Already, more than half of the tropical forests, which contain roughly half of all land species, are gone. Sixty percent of primate species, our biological cousins, are now heading toward extinction by the middle of this century. Yet, still, every year we continue to destroy as much as ten million hectares of tropical forest – an amount equal to one soccer field every two to three seconds.[1]

Is big business to blame? Just the opposite, the chief executive officers of the world's leading transnational corporations (TNCs) are telling us: big business is saving, not destroying, our planet. As Paul Polman, CEO of the Anglo-Dutch consumer goods company Unilever, remarked: "We are entering a very interesting period of history where the responsible business world is running ahead of the politicians."[2]

Pledging sustainability

The ambition of big business to protect our planet would seem boundless. To stop climate change, Nike says it is pursuing "sustainable innovation – a powerful strategy that drives us to dream bigger and get better." Monsanto says it is a "leader in innovative and sustainable agriculture," with a "simple mission": to "provide tools for farmers to help nourish the growing global population and help preserve the Earth for people, plants, wildlife and communities." Until recently even Volkswagen was saying it was aspiring by 2018 "to be the world's most successful and fascinating automobile manufacturer – and the leading light when it comes to sustainability."[3]

TNCs such as Coca-Cola and Pepsi are now competing to proclaim their enthusiasm. "Sustainability is the pivot for where we want to go – how we want to structure our processes, our thinking, our investments," declared Coca-Cola's CEO in 2010. "Companies like PepsiCo have a tremendous opportunity – as well as a responsibility – to not only make a profit, but to do so in a way that makes a difference in the world," said Pepsi's CEO in 2016.[4]

Only big business, the CEOs are telling anyone who will listen, has the power – and the determination – to make the hard decisions necessary for sustainable development, or what they are increasingly describing as "sustainability." Pursuing sustainability is good business in a world of growing scarcity, goes the refrain. "Environmental sustainability," asserts Walmart, "has become an essential ingredient to doing business responsibly and successfully."[5]

The past decade has seen sweeping promises by the world's biggest corporations. Zero deforestation. Carbon neutrality. Zero water footprints. One hundred percent renewable energy. Zero waste to landfill. Fully responsible sourcing. One hundred percent conflict-free ingredients. Can Walmart and Volkswagen and Nike truly help save us from full-blown planetary instability by the end of this century? What about ExxonMobil and Toyota and Apple? Or Google and General Electric and Costco? Or McDonald's and Coca-Cola and Mattel? Or Starbucks and Monsanto and Nestlé?

Most governments and many NGOs are clearly hoping so, nodding along as these companies declare themselves to be "sustainability leaders," and loudly applauding industry-friendly solutions, such as certification, offsetting, and voluntary corporate social responsibility (CSR). Leading scholars are also seeing promising signs of change in the business world. "Rather than looking to government for solutions," argues Professor Andrew Hoffman of the University of Michigan, "many businesses are taking responsibility for climate change seriously and changing the system on their own."[6]

Can these companies, as the world pledged in the 2015 Paris Agreement on Climate Change, really help keep global warming from exceeding 1.5°C? Or help end overfishing, deforestation, and biodiversity loss? Or help stop the depletion of fresh water? Or help curb plastic and chemical pollution?

Total Destruction?

Big-business sustainability

The world's biggest corporations deserve credit for changing some practices in response to the escalating global environmental crisis. Yet, as I argue in this book, trusting them to lead sustainability efforts is like trusting arsonists to be our firefighters. Here and there, they are extinguishing a fire or two, at times even relishing the task. But, compelled by their structure and purpose to pursue profits and growth at any cost, at every opportunity they are also setting new fires, all the while gesturing excitedly at areas doused in CSR to distract from the flames rising all around them. One should not be fooled: when all is said and done, what companies like Walmart, Coca-Cola, and BP are doing in the name of sustainability is aiming to advance the prosperity of business, not the integrity of ecosystems or the quality of future life.

For me, sustainability is the quality of advancing social justice without irreparably degrading ecosystems or harming future life. I do not see this as a condition the world will one day attain, but rather an ideal that political systems need to strive for constantly, like those of liberty, freedom, and justice. Defined in this way, the pursuit of global sustainability aims to balance the ecological and socioeconomic needs of all life. And defined in this way attributes of a sustainable system must include resilience, structural integrity, and dynamic balance.

Yet this is not how big business understands sustainability. Defining sustainability as the pursuit of greater technological efficiency, less waste, and more recycling can reduce some of the damage from rapidly rising production and consumption. But it won't stop the forces of planetary destruction. Doing so will necessitate intergenerational equity, a respect for nature, a fair distribution of earth shares, and reasonable consumption: all of which, as I'll show in this book, big business is now steering us away from.

I must be careful, however, not to overstate my case. Domestic laws and policies certainly constrain the options and actions of business, and TNCs do not have free rein around the world. There are many instances where big business does not get its way; on occasion, TNCs lose political struggles outright.[7] Moreover, as we will see in later chapters, corporate sustainability is obviously doing some good, with CSR creating some opportunities to nudge along environmental reforms. In fact, this explains much of the power of CSR to enhance brand value and legitimize corporate self-governance. And clearly more and more business executives and middle managers have come to believe in the power of pursuing CSR as a way to balance a firm's financial obligations with its environmental and social duties.

At first glance the results of CSR and sustainability policies can even seem impressive. Walmart is recycling more cardboard and selling more jewelry certified as "ethical." Apple is doing more to monitor the standards of the firms supplying the components for its IPhones, IPads, and Mac computers. BP is making some progress in reducing methane emissions during the production of natural gas. Google is transitioning to renewable energy, heading toward zero waste to landfill from its data centers, and tracking deforestation and overfishing. And Coca-Cola is offering more financing for water and wetlands conservation.

There is even some evidence of TNCs raising environmental standards in developing countries: what Ronie Garcia-Johnson memorably described as "exporting environmentalism" when explaining the consequences of big American chemical companies moving into Mexico and Brazil.[8] And there is some evidence of transnational mining, timber, and agrifood companies offering more benefits to communities in developing countries, such as funding schools and medical clinics.

Almost certainly, without such efforts the global

environmental crisis would be escalating at an even faster rate. Nor is there any question that most CSR and sustainability managers – and even a few CEOs – are genuinely committed to sustainability, as they understand it. Yet, the question animating this book is not, "Is big business CSR and sustainability doing bits of good here and there?" There has already been an avalanche of books claiming to find gains across a wide range of firms, countries, and sectors.[9]

My question is more ambitious in scope and one that, intriguingly, is rarely asked: "Is big business going to destroy the earth by the end of this century?" My starting answer is "no," at least not *completely*, as corporate self-interest, governmental policy, democratic processes, community resistance, the environmental movement, and the resilience of the earth itself will prevent total destruction. But my follow-up is important: unless states and civil societies do far more to rein in the rising power of big business over world politics and consumer cultures, big business *is* going to destroy *vast areas* of the earth's forests, oceans, lands, species, air, and atmosphere. Our planet will still exist; however, it will be a far more perilous place for all life.

Total Destruction?

Better than nothing?

At this point you might be ready to shrug and push back, "Well, corporate sustainability is a start; and it is certainly better than doing nothing at all." And, for sure, you would be correct. But, again, to be clear, I'm not suggesting that CSR and sustainability policies have no value for improving the environmental and social performance of big business. Nor am I suggesting that companies like Walmart or Unilever are not on occasion supporting higher environmental standards or better transnational environmental governance: they clearly are. Rather, I'm arguing that the voluntary, self-interested sustainability policies and strategies of big business will never aggregate into the systemic and transformative change necessary to stop the global environmental crisis from continuing to escalate, as these policies and strategies do not have the innate capacity to restrain the compulsion of big business to extract profits, exploit nature, and expand operations – and lay waste to the earth along the way.

Of course, the world's biggest TNCs are not solely responsible for the escalating global environmental crisis, as we will see when surveying this crisis in Chapter 5. There are many interacting and reinforcing forces at play. These include the legacies of imperialism and colonialism as well as the parochial politics arising out of a world order of sovereign states. They include the caustic nature of international trade, development financing, and capitalism itself. They include the ill will and corrupt ways of political leaders and cronies around the world. And they include the indifference, ignorance, and greed of more than 7.5 billion people – up from three billion in 1960. Yet the world's biggest TNCs, as I'll argue in this book, have a particularly great responsibility for causing the global environmental crisis to escalate, with their CSR and sustainability claims doing as much to obfuscate as to help.

At every turn, as this book will show, the same TNCs espousing CSR and sustainability continue to strive to minimize regulations, fees, and taxes (or seek subsidies). As law professor Joel Bakan tells us, a "corporation" is legally constructed to pursue profits and self-interest with the morality of a charming psychopath, never truly worrying about the consequences for others.[10] This helps explain why, as the Austrian Chancellor Christian Kern lamented in 2016 when expressing his frustration with Amazon and Starbucks, "Every Viennese cafe, every sausage stand pays more tax in Austria than a multinational corporation."[11]

Most often corporations pursue self-interest

through lobbying and lawyers. They finance political campaigns, probe for policy loopholes, and use the courts to bend rules in their favor. And they sow scientific uncertainty and public confusion by funding industry-friendly "research" and by disseminating misinformation.

Constantly seeking more power over markets, rule-makers, and competitors, the world's biggest companies are growing bigger and bigger, sometimes by acquiring and merging for mutual gain, sometimes by attacking and counterattacking in hostile takeovers. These companies are also frequently willing to break the law to gain a competitive edge, perhaps by bribing officials or perhaps by devising a scheme to evade auditors, certifiers, and regulators. The secret strategy by Volkswagen to install software in at least eleven million diesel cars to "defeat" emissions testing is just one of many examples over the past decade (Chapter 4 provides details).

Such behavior, however, only partly explains why big business, left to self-govern, will destroy so much of our natural world by the end of this century. Significantly, big business remains a driver of, not a solution for, three of the most potent forces underlying the escalating global environmental crisis: rising rates of excessive consumption; rising rates of wasteful consumption; and rising rates of unequal consumption. These forces are powering "overconsumption," understood as consumption that exceeds the capacity of the earth to regenerate natural systems and retain biological dynamism (Chapter 5 offers a full definition). Rising rates of overconsumption, as Chapter 5 details, is increasingly displacing the environmental and social costs of everyday living onto the world's poorest regions and most fragile ecosystems, as well as into the future: what one can think of as "ecological shadows of consumption."[12]

Certainly, big business provides many valuable economic and social services. And, without doubt, discount retailers such as Walmart and Costco are offering more affordable food, clothing, and appliances for those less well off. We need more consumption; I would never want to suggest otherwise, given so many people still live in extreme poverty, and given the world population is racing toward ten billion by the middle of this century. Yet, if we're ever going to get a handle on the escalating global environmental crisis, we need to confront the fact that at every turn big business is fostering excessive, unequal, and wasteful consumption.

This is driving global consumption far above the capacity of nature to regenerate or absorb the garbage and chemicals. The advertising campaigns of big business are reorienting entire cultures – from Europe to China to India to Brazil – to maximize the consumption of global brands. Markets are being flooded with nondurable goods and plastic products, from throwaway furniture to disposable diapers. Fast-food chains and processed food companies are shifting consumer preferences toward high-fat, high-salt, and high-sugar diets, contributing to rising worldwide rates of obesity among both the rich and poor. Big agricultural firms are taking over smallholder lands to mass-produce crops and meat. Electronic and appliance companies are designing products for quick obsolescence and non-reparability. And automakers are extoling the virtues of trading in for the newest model.

The profits from the manufacturing of ever-higher rates of overconsumption are enhancing the financial power of corporations and the political influence of billionaires. To further extend this power, over the past ten years big business has been steadily gaining control over the framing and implementation of sustainability policies, a trend reinforced by the broader tendency of governments since the 1980s to deregulate, privatize, and free up the world economy for TNCs.

One consequence of the enhanced power of big business over sustainability discourses and policies has been to shift global environmental governance toward solutions friendly to big business: ones that are voluntary, market-based, growth-oriented, industrial-scale, trade-focused, and profit-reinforcing. Such governance is opening up some opportunities to increase recycling and energy efficiency, reduce packaging and waste, and raise the standards of corporate suppliers. It is providing some funding for conservation. And it is offering some opportunities for environmental NGOs and community groups to work alongside big business. But, as we will see time and again in this book, the priority on corporate interests is causing environmental gains to rebound into even greater ecological pressures as these companies reinvest savings to expand production, increase sales, enhance profits, and bring untested substitutes to market.

Big business

The concept of "big business," you might reasonably push back, washes out important differences in the initiatives and consequences of particular companies. Definitely, public companies with global brands are responding more proactively to sustainability demands than private companies without much public profile. Technology firms like Google and Apple are certainly doing more to embrace renewable energy than oil companies like Chevron or Phillips 66. And for sure the ecological consequences of the agrochemical company Monsanto are very different from the mining company Glencore. Even the effects of Subway and Starbucks are somewhat different in North America than in Asia.

Contrasting the consequences of big-box retailers like Home Depot and Office Depot with fast-food chains like KFC and McDonald's would undoubtedly yield insights into the different ways CSR is playing out. So would comparing similar companies across political jurisdictions – say contrasting the environmental consequences of the automakers Volkswagen, Toyota, and General Motors across the jurisdictions of Europe, North America, and Asia. And so would delving deeply into the motives, actions, and consequences of firms such as the outdoor clothing company Patagonia, which describes itself as "an activist company" "using business to inspire and implement solutions to the environmental crisis."[13] Still, as I hope to demonstrate by the end of this book, setting aside the many differences across TNCs and analyzing big business as a singular force offers unique insights into why the environmental crisis is escalating, why overconsumption is rising, and why corporate self-governance is never going to solve this crisis.

Even if you accept the conceptual value of the term big business, you might still be wondering: "Is big business really any worse than small- or medium-sized business?" Would it perhaps make sense to retitle this book, "*Will Capitalism Destroy Our Planet?*" After all, as Karl Marx (1818–83) had already illuminated back in the nineteenth century, capitalism spreads like a cancer through cultures and nature. Small business, it is true, can be just as corrosive as big business, as we can see with logging, cattle ranching, soy production, and palm oil plantations in the tropics.

There are, however, good reasons for focusing on big business rather than on capitalism or all business. For one, many others have already exposed the destructive nature of capitalism on the global environment, such as Naomi Klein in *This Changes Everything*, Christopher Wright and Daniel Nyberg in *Climate Change, Capitalism, and Corporations*, and Jason Moore in *Capitalism in the Web of Life*. More importantly, however, shining a torchlight on big business allows us to see the dominant destroyers in a capitalist system so hegemonic as to seem nameless and blameless. By doing so in a short, essay-

16

style book, I hope to offer an especially vivid picture of the consequences of big business over the past decade, aiming to expose to much-needed scrutiny the increasingly common assertion by big business that it is not destroying our planet, but is instead transforming capitalism toward sustainability – a false claim that more and more state and nonprofit leaders are obviously coming to trust.

The chapters ahead

As we will see over the course of this book, the power of big business both to protect and destroy the planet is rising. Big business is not only gaining more and more control over global supply chains, national economies, and consumer cultures, as Chapter 2 will show, it is also gaining more and more influence over the discourses, agendas, and governance mechanisms of sustainability, as Chapter 3 will review.

More and more CEOs of big business, as Chapter 3 discusses, are arguing that the rising power of TNCs is offering increasing opportunities for CSR to promote global sustainability. According to these CEOs, nowadays there are especially good opportunities to create incentives and supply technologies to help raise the standards of their hundreds of thousands of suppliers. There is some truth to this claim. And it is understandable why so many people want to believe in corporate sustainability, given the capacity, when big business wants, to enforce its will around the world. As Chapter 4 will reveal, however, there is a dark underbelly to the business of CSR, where it is simultaneously concealing illegalities, obfuscating accountability, and legitimizing the increasing concentration of power and wealth within corporations.

Moreover, as Chapter 5 outlines, even the corporations with the best CSR practices are powerful forces causing unsustainable production and overconsumption to escalate. And, as the chapter further documents, climate change, deforestation, chemical contamination, land degradation, ocean depletion, and plastic pollution are all getting worse as the ecological shadows of overconsumption intensify. This is deeply concerning, as states and NGOs are increasingly turning to these same corporations to govern us out of the global environmental crisis, shifting governance away from regulatory mechanisms and societal oversight and toward voluntary, corporate self-regulation aiming to profit from this crisis.

Global environmentalism, as both a movement

and philosophy, has been a powerful counterforce to consumer capitalism over the past half-century. And, as I discuss in Chapter 6, environmentalism continues to be highly influential. Still, as I argue in this concluding chapter, those governments, NGOs, and consumers conceding authority and offering legitimacy to CSR should be far more wary of business partnerships, philanthropy, and financing, and far more alert to the post-truth politics underlying what big business is calling sustainability.

Voluntary codes of conduct and feel-good declarations of responsibility are never going to turn big business into a force of social justice and planetary sustainability. Any chance of stopping big business from destroying much of the earth will require governments and societies to reorient global environmental politics to reduce – and then restrain – the power of big business. Doing so is increasingly urgent, as the exact opposite is now happening, with the financial, political, and cultural power of big business rising at an ever-quickening clip.

2

The Rising Power of Big Business

Since World War II, global change has been accelerating like a Formula One car screeching out of a pit stop. The globalization of big business has been an especially powerful engine of change.

McDonald's and Starbucks have transformed food cultures. Walmart and Amazon have altered the way people shop. Nike and Christian Dior have changed the way people dress. Apple and Microsoft have reoriented the way people work and play. And Volkswagen and Delta Air Lines have changed the way people travel. Meanwhile, Royal Dutch Shell and Glencore have mined the earth for oil and minerals, Cargill and Monsanto have reshaped global agriculture, and Dow Chemical and Dupont have greased the moving parts of the world economy.

All around the world these transnational corporations have bought up plantations, logging and mineral rights, local businesses, and factories. But, unlike in the early post-war period, today much of the power of TNCs comes through their global supply chains, which link first-tier, second-tier, and third-tier suppliers through purchasing contracts, technological support, and financing arrangements. Walmart alone has more than 100,000 suppliers. This flexible, dynamic business model, while sacrificing some of the control of direct ownership, has allowed the world's biggest corporations to extend their influence much further and much deeper into the global processes of extraction, production, and consumption.

These corporations have gained extraordinary financial power. America's top 500 corporations now account for two-thirds of the country's gross domestic product (GDP). Of the world's top 100 revenue generators in 2015, 69 were companies and 31 were states. That year the top twenty companies alone turned over US$3.4 trillion in revenues.

The growing dominance of big business in the world economy is also enriching corporate owners and executives. Consider the number of billionaires, up fifteen-fold from 1986 to 2017 (from 140 to 2043). Together, Forbes calculates these billionaires were worth around US$7.7 trillion in 2017. Even this staggeringly high figure likely underestimates the total wealth of the super-rich, as many conceal assets in tax havens and secret accounts (the leaking of the Panama Papers in 2015 gave the public a rare glimpse into these practices). The resulting inequality even in terms of legal wealth is stunning. At the start of 2017 the top eight of these billionaires held as much wealth as the bottom half of humanity.[1]

With this increasing financial power has also come increasing power over political systems and cultural understandings, with waterfalls of money cascading into political parties, lobbying campaigns, advertising, and branding. How did big business come to gain so much influence over our lives?

The emergence of TNCs

The beginning of corporations with wealth and power as great as small states extends back to the seventeenth century when European monarchs awarded monopolies to trading firms to plunder the "New World." Britain's East India Company, founded in 1600, is one of the most infamous. But there were many others. There were the Dutch East India Company (founded in 1602) and the Dutch West India Company (founded in 1621). There was the French East India Company (founded in

The Rising Power of Big Business

1664). And there were Britain's Hudson's Bay Company (founded in 1670) and Britain's Royal African Company (founded in 1660/1672). These companies did far more than just pillage the New World for slaves, spices, cotton, silk, tea, timber, furs, gold, silver, and opium. They also waged wars, spread pandemics (such as smallpox, measles, and influenza), and razed the ecological and social landscapes of Africa, the Asia-Pacific, and the Americas.[2]

The modern transnational corporation – or what some call "multinational corporations" (MNCs) and others call "multinational enterprises" (MNEs) – surfaced out of this violent exploitation of the New World. The number of firms working across multiple countries began to rise in the late nineteenth and early twentieth centuries. One example is Lever Brothers, Britain's leading soapmaker in 1900. Over the next twenty years the company would continue to expand, mass-producing soaps, advertising heavily, buying coconut plantations in Melanesia, acquiring trading firms in Africa, and taking over competitors. By the beginning of the 1920s the company controlled nearly three-quarters of England's soap market. In 1929, Lever Brothers would then combine with the Dutch firm Margarine Unie to form Unilever: at the time, one of the biggest mergers ever.

The roots of many of America's iconic TNCs also extend to this period. The Coca-Cola Company goes back to an Atlanta pharmacist concocting the first Coca-Cola drink in 1886. Its main competitor, the Pepsi-Cola Company, traces its beginnings to a North Carolina pharmacist mixing the first Pepsi drink in 1893, with the company forming in 1902. American oil companies also surfaced during this time, with a signature moment being John D. Rockefeller's founding of the Standard Oil Company in 1870 (a precursor of today's ExxonMobil).

The shift toward mass production would help many American companies grow quickly during the first quarter of the twentieth century. After forming in 1903 the Ford Motor Company, for instance, would mass produce over fifteen million Model T's from 1908 to 1927. Over this time Goodyear Tire and Rubber Company, after starting up in Ohio in 1898, would emerge as the world's biggest rubber corporation. Its crosstown rival Firestone Tire and Rubber Company (founded in 1900) also grew into a global powerhouse as a tire supplier for Henry Ford's Model T's, in 1926 acquiring a vast rubber plantation in Liberia (notorious for human rights violations since then).[3]

The Rising Power of Big Business

The post World War II explosion

The growth in the size and number of TNCs began to pick up speed after 1945. There were many reasons. The American economy was booming and global markets were expanding. Technological innovation began to accelerate. And transnational production costs began to fall, as American, European, and later Japanese and Chinese firms became more efficient at extracting natural resources and exploiting workers in developing countries.

The 1950s saw the emergence of restaurant franchising and fast-food chains. The McDonald's Corporation under Ray Kroc led the way after opening its first franchise restaurant in Illinois in 1955 (although Dick and Mac McDonald opened the first McDonald's restaurant in 1940). When the McDonald's Corporation went public in 1965, the company had 700 restaurants across the United States. By the end of the 1970s there were 5,000 restaurants around the world; by the mid-1990s, there were 20,000. Today, there are around 36,000 restaurants across more than one hundred countries. Other American fast-food chains also grew at record rates during this time, including Subway (now around 45,000 outlets), Starbucks (around 25,000), KFC (around 20,000), Burger

King (around 15,000), and Pizza Hut (around 13,000).

The American Sam Walton would also revolutionize retailing after opening the first Walmart in 1962 in Arkansas. In retrospect, his core idea seems rather simple: maximize profits by maximizing sales (rather than by trying to maximize profits per sale). To propel sales, he slashed his prices, cutting his costs to the bone to still retain a tiny profit margin on each sale. He set up in no-frills, large warehouses in low-rent areas, buying in bulk, and lining his shelves with discounted goods. And he hired part-time, non-unionized workers, paying low wages and minimizing benefits. He then reinvested his profits to expand, driving other retailers out of business and further enhancing his power to squeeze out even better deals on his bulk orders.[4]

Walmart's sales soared under this business model. Annual revenues hit US$1 billion by the late 1970s. Before long, other retailers were building upon his idea, such as Costco (1976, beginning as Price Club) and Home Depot (1979). During the 1980s and 1990s, however, Walmart's revenues climbed far above any other big-box retailer. Today, the company employs over 2.3 million people across more than 11,500 stores and retail clubs. Revenues in 2016 (or, what Walmart calls fiscal year 2017, ending January 31) were US$486 billion, making Walmart yet again the world's biggest company by annual revenue turnover – also true in the previous three years. And the company has no plans to slow down expansion.

Already in 2016, Walmart's revenues were equal to what the top sixty-five American firms together turned over in 1975. No other company has come close to Walmart's revenues in recent years. Its revenues in 2016 were more than US$170 billion ahead of the world's second biggest company, China's utility firm, State Grid. Its revenues far surpassed America's second biggest company, Berkshire Hathaway – by a tidy US$262 billion. And impressively, that year it turned over US$350 billion more in revenue than its nearest retailing competitor, Amazon, US$367 billion more in revenue than Costco, and US$391 billion more in revenue than Home Depot.

Even with the rise of Walmart, however, companies dealing in oil and gas still remain at the core of big business. China's State Grid, Sinopec Group (an oil company), and China National Petroleum ranked second, third, and fourth respectively on Fortune's list of the 500 biggest companies in 2016, while Royal Dutch Shell, ExxonMobil, and BP ranked seventh, tenth, and twelfth respectively. Automakers also remain powerful revenue generators. Toyota sat atop the automakers in 2016, ranking as the fifth biggest company, one place ahead of Volkswagen (Daimler was 17th, General Motors was 18th, and Ford was 21st).

Over the past half-century, however, tens of thousands of other TNCs have joined these oil and auto companies on the world stage. American companies such as Apple, Amazon, Hewlett-Packard, Microsoft, and Nike became well-known global brands. So too did many European TNCs, such as Britain's Tesco and France's Christian Dior. And so, too, did Japanese TNCs, such as Hitachi, Sony, and Panasonic, as well as Korean TNCs, such as Samsung. The spectacular rise of Chinese companies since 2000 has brought yet another wave of powerful corporations, with Chinese firms accounting for more than one-fifth of the world's top 500 biggest companies in 2015. That year only the United States had more companies in the top 500, with 134 (Japan was third, with 52 firms).

These 500 leading companies have prodigious sway over the global economy, with their investment increasingly essential for economic and political stability in most of the world. We can see this in the sheer size of their annual revenue turnover, which in 2016 was US$27.7 trillion, with profits of US$1.5 trillion. The financial power of big business dominates even the US economy. The 500 largest companies headquartered in the USA, for instance, turned over US$12 trillion in revenues in 2015, accounting for two-thirds of America's GDP, employing nearly twenty-eight million people, and hauling in US$840 billion in profits. That year, Apple was the world's most profitable company, raking in US$53 billion (a record for Apple). The following year the top five hundred US companies were even more profitable, pulling in US$890 billion, although Apple's profits were lower (US$46 billion).[5]

The spectacular increase since World War II in the sales and profits of the world's biggest companies partly reflects their increasing capacity to extend their reach through global supply chains. It also reflects, however, their growing capacity to expand markets through branding and advertising, at first in developed countries, and since 2000 increasingly across emerging and developing economics.

Re-engineering consumer cultures

Branding and advertising not only aim to sell products, but also mold cultural values, desires, and frames. "Everything we do at Porter Novelli," the international advertising agency pitches to prospective clients on its website, "is designed to achieve one goal: to transform the opinions, beliefs and behaviors of those who matter most to our clients."

Advertisers bombard TV viewers, social media users, and radio listeners; they slip messages into songs, museum displays, and video games; they embed subliminal images into movies, teenage fiction, and cartoons. Of course, the re-engineering of consumer cultures to increase demand for a particular brand goes back hundreds of years. In 1906, for instance, Lever Brothers was advertising the power of its "Lifebuoy Soap" to "clean" and "disinfect" the world to "Save Lives". Yet since World War II advertising and branding have gained an influence far greater than ever before in history.

Worldwide, companies with global brands are spending around US$500 billion a year on advertising.[6] The financial value of today's brands reveals some of the payback from this investment. Forbes ranks Apple as the world's most valuable brand – worth more than US$154 billion in 2016 – far ahead of the next four, Google, Microsoft, Coca-Cola, and Facebook.

One sign of the influence of advertising and branding is the increasing similarity of consumerism across cultures. Every culture now offers a greater variety of food, clothes, and consumer products. Yet the options have become increasingly homogenous: an abundance of sushi, tacos, pizza, and hamburgers for all. The great rise in per capita consumption of salt and sugar is one indication of the growing homogeneity. Another is the steady rise in the global consumption of processed food ingredients, such as corn, wheat, soy, and palm oil.[7]

A glance at the McDonald's Corporation reveals the power of fast-food chains to reshape diets. Every second McDonald's sells around 75 burgers: for a grand total of well over 100 billion since 1970. Americans still eat the most McDonald's burgers. But Japan is now the second biggest consumer, with around 3,000 McDonald's restaurants, followed by China with around 2,000 outlets. Such expansion helps explain the global rise in per capita meat consumption since World War II, with residents in places like the United States now consuming on average more than 200 pounds a year. And such expansion helps explain the steady increase in the number of farmed cattle (1.5 billion), pigs (1 billion), goats (1 billion), and chickens (20 billion), as well as the surge in demand for animal feed made from soy and corn.

The case of Procter & Gamble, the world's biggest consumer goods company, further reveals the power of retailers and brands to reshape consumption. P&G, which spends US$9 to US$10 billion a year on advertising, had twenty brands worth more than US$1 billion in 2016 – including Pampers, Tide, Crest, Gillette, and Duracell. Advertising does not come cheaply: a thirty-second slot during the 2017 Super Bowl cost around US$5 million, about twice as much as during the 2007 Super Bowl and ten times as much as in 1985. But this price tag did not deter P&G's Mr. Clean, Febreze, or Tide brands from running ads.

Nor did the cost of a 2017 Super Bowl advertisement deter automakers. Ford, Audi, and Fiat ran ads. So did Chrysler, Mercedes, and Buick. And so did Honda, Lexus, Hyundai, and Kia. Over the past half-century no product has come to re-engineer physical landscapes and cultures quite like the automobile. Most simply, we can see this in the sharp rise in the number of cars, sport utility vehicles (SUVs), and trucks on the world's roads: from 250 million in 1970 to one billion in 2010 to around 1.5 billion today. And industry analysts are expecting the number of motor vehicles to double by 2050 as demand continues to soar in countries such as China and India.

The Rising Power of Big Business

The concentration of wealth and power

Of course, the billionaires of business have long wielded great political power, as we see in the United States with Cornelius Vanderbilt (1794–1877), Andrew Carnegie (1835–1919), John D. Rockefeller (1839–1937), and Henry Ford (1863–1947). What is different today, however, is the proliferation of billionaires and the deepening of the economic and societal power of big business across just about every culture. The coming to power of Donald Trump as President of the United States in 2017 is symbolic of the rising political power of the world's billionaires. Yet the power of big business goes far deeper than the rise of right-wing billionaire populism.

Ruling parties in democracies have become indebted to the owners and CEOs of big business. Authoritarian governments have also come to rely on the support of big business to calm dissent within the middle classes. The agendas and rules of bureaucracies, financial institutions, and banking have also come to echo the priorities of big business. International NGOs have come to rely on business charity, celebrity-business sponsorships, cobranding partnerships, and cause-marketing to fund campaigns and pay overheads. Even public universities have gradually come under the influence of big business, with corporate philanthropy now core to the funding of many leading public universities.[8]

And the concentration of wealth and power at the top of the business world is only increasing. The United States alone saw over US$10 trillion in mergers from 2008 to 2017, with 2015 a record year for the number of mergers. Hillary Clinton, writing in 2015, was highly critical of the increasingly monopolistic power of America's top companies since the mid-1990s. "Rather than offering better products for lower prices," she argued, "they are using their power to raise prices, limit choices for consumers, lower wages for workers, and hold back competition from startups and small businesses."[9]

The growing concentration of corporate power is equally true globally. "Corporate power is now more concentrated and operates ever further beyond human control," noted David Korten, after surveying the landscape twenty years after publishing his 1995 bestselling book, *When Corporations Rule the World*. "Its exercise is more reckless. Its political domination is more complete," he concluded.[10]

Consider for a moment the increasing corporate control of global agriculture. In the 1990s around six hundred companies sold the bulk of the world's fertilizer, pesticides, and seeds. Yet in recent years a handful of well-known TNCs – ones such as Monsanto, Bayer, Dow, DuPont, ChemChina, and Syngenta – have come to dominate these markets. In India, for instance, Monsanto's genetically modified cotton seeds accounted for more than ninety percent of total cotton seed sales in 2015. And these companies are continuing to fight for even more control, with Dow Chemical and DuPont starting a process to merge in 2015, with Bayer beginning a process to acquire Monsanto in 2016, and with ChemChina moving to buy Syngenta in 2017 (these deals were going through regulatory approval processes in 2017).

It is increasingly common for farmers, who once could choose from hundreds of varieties of seeds for each crop, now to have just a few to choose from. Not only are these seeds generally more expensive, but often they're genetically modified in ways that create dependencies on the company's fertilizers and pesticides. Terry Boehm, a farmer in Canada for more than thirty-five years, has no illusions about what has been going on. "Clearly, the focus for a long time has been greater and greater control of seeds," he said in 2016. "And if you control the seed, you control the food system. And you control people, ultimately." Worldwide, this trend toward ever-bigger agrifood corporations is having far-reaching social and environmental consequences. "From Africa and Asia to Latin America and the EU, corporate control over markets and supply chains is displacing millions of small-scale farmers" and causing widespread hunger and poverty, explains Adrian Bebb of Friends of the Earth Europe.[11]

The CEOs of big business are well aware of their rising power over global governance, and many are quick to acknowledge this, perhaps reflecting what some describe as "CEO narcissism."[12] "Today, businesses have much more power and impact than fifty or a hundred years ago, when the main impact came from decisions made by countries' leaders," explains Feike Sijbesma, the CEO of the Dutch chemical and pharmaceutical company, Royal DSM.[13]

"There is not a week goes by when I am not with policy makers," adds Unilever CEO Paul Polman. "This position gives me access to these people and then it is a responsibility to leverage that." Polman is not shy about expressing the need for big business to govern. "Governments are coming out of office almost on a weekly basis so the onus is on companies to lead the way."[14]

Many other CEOs are equally quick to accept

responsibility for leading sustainability. "Companies like ours do not have the barriers that some governments have in trying to do the right thing," explains Bob McDonald, the former CEO of Procter & Gamble. "Many large companies are bigger than countries," adds Indra Nooyi, CEO of PepsiCo. "With our market cap, we are the thirty-seventh-largest republic in the world. And we have global governance, which many countries don't, or many regions don't. I think we have to do our part to bring our heft and the fact that we have global governance to find ways to improve society wherever we are."[15]

In part, then, the rising influence of big business over sustainability discourses and practices comes from the growing capacity of TNCs to shape global politics, the world economy, and societies, including nonprofit organizations. However, as the next chapter discusses, part of the rising influence of big business comes from a strategy to gain more power to structure the rules and institutions of global governance by framing – and ultimately trying to control – sustainability discourses and CSR practices.

3

The Business of CSR

The concept of corporate social responsibility emerged as a way to try to balance a company's financial obligations to owners and shareholders with political and public demands to contribute directly to the wellbeing of the economy and society. It began as charitable giving and employee programs. But over the course of the twentieth century, as corporations sought ways to protect their reputations, mollify state regulators, and minimize the costs of social conflict, its meaning began to broaden to include the idea of corporations self-regulating to improve their transparency, consumer information, supplier practices, community engagement, and environmental management. Today, corporate executives commonly express the spirit of CSR as the voluntary pursuit of a "triple bottom line": financial, social, and environmental.

In theory, achieving this triple bottom line, which CSR managers like to point out may require going beyond what local laws require, will grow a company, serve the needs of a society, and do no lasting ecological harm. Advocates often describe this as a "win–win–win" strategy for achieving "sustainable development," generally defined along the lines of the United Nations' 1987 World Commission on Environment and Development: "development that meets the needs of the present without compromising the ability of future generations to meet their own needs."[1]

In practice, however, the consequences of pursuing CSR rarely follow this reassuring logic. As this chapter shows, the theory of CSR does seem to work reasonably well when CSR is aiming to improve production efficiencies, reduce operating costs, pry open markets, or offer competitive advantages. And looking over the past decade, CSR and sustainability policies have clearly been improving the environmental and social performance of some aspects of some firms.

Yet, as later chapters will document, gains are generally incremental and rarely shift a firm's total consequences in any meaningful way; meanwhile, as we will see in this chapter, the corporate discourse around the wins of triple bottom line management wildly exaggerates the capacity of big business to promote planetary sustainability. This embellished discourse serves three strategic purposes: to soften criticism and generate praise for big business, including from human rights and environmental groups; to enhance corporate power over sustainability governance; and to justify a regulatory setting amenable to maximizing production, profits, and sales. This is the real business of CSR.

CSR as a public relations strategy

During the 1970s, 1980s, and into the 1990s the CSR branches of TNCs were mostly "greenwashing" business as usual with glossy brochures and philanthropic gifts. Today, at least in part, the CSR, philanthropy, and sustainability offices of every TNC – or what some firms now fold into a single unit in charge of "corporate responsibility" or "sustainability" or "citizenship" – still aim to protect corporate reputations, enhance brand value, and garner community support: what executives sometimes refer to as securing a "social license to operate."

Philanthropic initiatives offer scholarships, support research institutes and charities, and donate to hospitals and universities. Monsanto and ExxonMobil are typical. "Giving is a natural part of what we do," Monsanto tells us. Monsanto and the Monsanto Fund support agricultural research, youth organizations, and student bursa ries, in recent years totaling more than US$2 million a day in giving, according to the company. The Exxon Mobil Corporation and the ExxonMobil Foundation similarly support education, NGOs, community development, arts and culture, and gender equality, as well as specific programs, such as one to combat malaria. For 2016 the company estimated its total giving at US$204 million.[2]

The corporate discourse around sustainability can sound a lot like advertising. Just about every service, activity, and product is now marketed as "sustainable," as we see with the rhetoric of companies like BP and Coca-Cola. "Sustainability is at the heart of BP's strategy," reassures BP's CEO. "Our work on sustainable business practices not only helps to improve the lives of individuals and families across the Coca-Cola system," says the CEO of the Coca-Cola Company, "it also helps to strengthen the connections between our brands and the people who reach for them more than 1.9 billion times a day."[3]

Or look at McDonald's rhetoric. The company is

"helping to lead a global movement on beef sustainability" and is now on a "journey to sustainable beef," the McDonald's Corporation tells customers. How? Well, in the company's words, "every day all around the globe, McDonald's is putting people, processes and practices into place to make sustainability the new normal – for our business, society, and the world at large."[4]

What big business is not claiming to be ethical, responsible, and sustainable? The answer is none. And how often do the CSR and sustainability reports ignore a failure to meet a past commitment? The answer is all the time.

Still, there is more to CSR and sustainability policies than just philanthropy, upbeat messaging, triumphant declarations, shrewd marketing, and "corporate oxymorons" like "clean coal" and "safe cigarettes."[5] Especially since the mid-2000s the pursuit of environmental sustainability has become an increasingly valuable strategy to achieve traditional business gains.

CSR *as a business strategy*

Nowadays, CSR goes well beyond greenwashing. In particular, what corporations often call "environmental sustainability" is more accurately understood as "eco-business," a concept Jane Lister and I coined in our book, *Eco-Business*. Shaping the discourses of environmental management to improve corporate image and reputations is certainly a big part of eco-business. And so is reducing the risk of becoming a target of activist campaigns, community uprisings, or state regulators.

But the eco-business of just about every TNC now goes much further. It also involves putting in place tighter controls to manage risks and uncertainties within global supply chains. To gain more control firms are establishing codes of conduct and environmental reporting programs for subsidiaries and suppliers. Apple, for example, has a "Supplier Code of Conduct" that "requires" suppliers "to provide safe working conditions, treat workers with dignity and respect, act fairly and ethically, and use environmentally responsible practices wherever they make products or perform services for Apple."[6] Increasingly, TNCs like Apple are also auditing suppliers and subcontractors for compliance with these codes, including by hiring third-party inspectors.

Eco-business also involves participating in certification organizations and marketing certified products. The consumer good company Unilever – with brands such as Dove, Hellmann's, and

Lipton – has been a leader in setting up business-friendly environmental certification. The company, for instance, was a founding member of three of the world's biggest nongovernmental organizations now certifying products as "sustainable": the Forest Stewardship Council (FSC), established in 1993 to certify wood products; the Marine Stewardship Council (MSC), formed in 1996 to certify wild seafood; and the Roundtable on Sustainable Palm Oil (RSPO), established in 2004 to certify palm oil.

Today, the FSC logo is stamped on eight to ten percent of the world's traded timber, with companies such as Home Depot and Office Depot selling large amounts of FSC-certified furniture, lumber, and paper. The MSC logo appears on around ten percent of the annual global wild seafood catch (by weight), with companies such as Walmart, Costco, and Carrefour now selling significant quantities. And the RSPO is certifying around twenty percent of the world's palm oil as sustainable, with companies such as Ferrero, PepsiCo, Nestlé, and Procter & Gamble major customers.

Eco-business further involves implementing smart-packaging – from using lighter plastics to thinner cardboard – to decrease production and transportation costs. Coca-Cola in Britain, for instance, reduced its overall packaging by fifteen percent from 2007 to

2017. Eco-business also includes expanding waste and recycling programs to reduce expenditures and gain more control over the quality of inputs. Coca-Cola in Britain is again a reasonable example, with its plastic bottles now made from twenty five percent recycled materials. The Coca-Cola Company, along with companies such as Mars, Danone, PepsiCo, and Unilever, have also sponsored a global initiative by the Ellen MacArthur Foundation (launched in 2016) that is aiming for a fivefold increase in global reuse and recycling of plastic packaging (up from around fourteen percent in 2017).[7]

As Lister and I argue, however, as TNCs trumpet their recent environmental gains and sponsorships, we need to be very careful to keep in mind that eco-business is ultimately a strategy to gain competitive advantages in a world spiralling into ever-greater environmental crisis. At its core it is endeavoring to secure increasingly scarce natural resources. It is striving to cut operating costs. It is seeking to enhance quality controls within supply chains, better manage risks, and reach into new markets. It is working to improve corporate images and retain a social license to operate. And it is aiming to enhance brand values, increase profits and sales, and ultimately grow the company into an even bigger and more powerful organization.[8]

It would be a mistake, however, to dismiss eco-business as the same across all companies. Some companies are doing more and going further. And some CEOs and many CSR managers clearly believe in the power of corporate sustainability to do great good: to produce, in the language of business, "shared value" for the economy and society.[9] Assuming that CSR philanthropy and eco-business are merely serving the interests of business would be an even bigger mistake. On some measures these efforts are definitely improving some environmental and social conditions.

At times, these efforts can even seem to hold a potential for gains far greater than those possible through state regulation or nonprofit organizations. This is important to acknowledge, as the capacity for real – and seemingly far-reaching – gains explains much of the power of eco-business. This helps explain its power to enhance the images and reputations of big business. It helps explain its power to produce significant competitive advantages for those companies leading the charge. And it helps explain its power to convince states and NGOs that voluntary self-regulation is an efficient and effective governance pathway toward global sustainability.

The Business of CSR

Walmart: "Save Money. Live Better"

Consider Walmart's sustainability strategy since 2005. Wading through Walmart's CSR and sustainability reports since then, it is easy to forget that the company's expansionist business model is in many ways the antithesis of what most people would think of as progress toward sustainability. To cut operating costs, as we saw in Chapter 2, Walmart pays low wages, minimizes employee benefits, prohibits unions, and runs no-frills outlets. To discount its prices, it bargains hard, buying cheap, disposable, nondurable goods in bulk. And to expand sales it drives smaller retailers near its stores into bankruptcy. This business model, as we will explore in Chapter 5, is propelling unsustainable consumption around the world, which in turn is driving the overharvesting of natural resources, the depletion of nonrenewable resources, the degradation from manufacturing, the pollution from long-distance transportation, and the overfilling of planetary sinks.

Walmart's business model helps explain why the gains from the sustainability and responsibility policies of big business are not adding up to global solutions. Still, there is some truth to Walmart's claim of being a leader among TNCs professing to be sustainable and responsible. Many analysts credit its 2005 "sustainability commitment" for shifting big business toward using CSR and sustainability programs to compete for business advantages, rather than seeing them as primarily public relations and damage control tools. Since 2005 Walmart's sustainability strategy has done wonders for its reputation and brand image, with authors such as the Pulitzer-prize winner Edward Humes going as far as calling Walmart a "force of nature," leading a "green revolution."[10]

On some measures Walmart is greening its operations. Since 2005 Walmart has become the world's biggest organic grocer. It has implemented policies to promote more responsible sourcing of food, including from smaller farms, organic growers, and agricultural producers with fair-trade and environmental certifications. And Walmart stores and Sam's Clubs are now selling seafood certified by the Marine Stewardship Council, paper certified by the Forest Stewardship Council, and jewelry certified as ethical and conflict free.

Additionally, every year, as part of a commitment to reduce food waste, Walmart is donating hundreds of millions of meals worth of food to hunger-relief organizations. The company also has philanthropic programs to support communities after natural disasters, as well as promote veterans and women in retailing. This philanthropy adds up. In terms of cash and in-kind donations, for fiscal year 2016 (ending January 31) Walmart and the Walmart Foundation gave away US$1.4 billion.[11]

Walmart's sustainability strategy has also clearly helped the company to improve its energy efficiency, waste management, and recycling. The energy efficiency of its US fleet of trucks doubled from 2005 to 2015, saving the company around US$1 billion. Stores across the USA have installed solar panels, with Target the only company in the USA with more installed capacity in 2016. Walmart is now diverting three-quarters of the glass, plastic, paper, cardboard, and food waste from its global operations from going into landfills. And worldwide the company reduced its annual plastic bag waste by ten billion bags from 2007 to 2013.[12]

Walmart's sustainability strategy has also helped its suppliers to reduce inefficiencies, waste, and greenhouse gas emissions. And Walmart is pushing for even more changes here. In collaboration with environmental NGOs, for instance, in 2017 Walmart launched what it calls "Project Gigaton," a "toolkit" to help its suppliers reduce greenhouse gas emissions by a gigaton (1 billion tons) from 2015 to 2030.

Sustainability and responsibility strategies similar to Walmart's are also offering other global corporations opportunities to enhance brand value, improve efficiencies, cut costs, expand markets, and govern supply chains more efficiently and effectively, both environmentally and financially. They are also helping to legitimize self-regulation and self-governance by TNCs.

Look at the praise heaped on Walmart's Project Gigaton by the Worldwide Fund for Nature/World Wildlife Fund (WWF) and the Environmental Defense Fund (EDF). "Project Gigaton is a testament to the transformative impact that leaders of industry can have on our greatest common challenges," declared Carter Roberts, President of WWF in the USA. "As more companies follow in the footsteps of Walmart and their suppliers, we can achieve the critical mass needed to address climate change."

"A challenge like Project Gigaton will catalyze leadership and innovative solutions around the globe," added EDF President Fred Krupp. "Forward-looking companies like Walmart, and the suppliers that will join them, know that our economy and our planet can – and must – thrive together. Consumers deserve both, and these businesses are leading the way."[13]

Taking over responsibility

TNCs do not hesitate to declare their willingness to take responsibility for advancing sustainability. "We have a responsibility to lead," explained Alexandra Palt, director of CSR and sustainability at L'Oreal, the world's biggest cosmetics company. "Each year, 1.7 million children die from pollution; people are starving because of climate change. We can't wait until everybody is on board to start changing our practices."[14]

Nor do TNCs hesitate to declare their enthusiasm for taking the lead across every political jurisdiction. "Every single person in the Coca-Cola system, we believe wholeheartedly that we cannot have a sustainable business and a growing business unless we have sustainable communities," stated Muhtar Kent, then CEO of Coca-Cola. "We have a role and responsibility to play in helping to create sustainable communities, whether it is a village in Kenya or a metropolis like Mexico City."[15]

Taking over responsibility for sustainability has strategic value beyond just the competitive advantages arising from the savings and efficiencies of eco-business. As ethics professor Allison Marchildon explains well, "the nature of the responsibility" does not require "fixing the problems" as defined by states or societies, but instead "gives corporations the political power to define what our public problems are and how they should be fixed."[16] Most significantly, big business is using its growing power over sustainability to steer NGO discourses, governmental agendas, and global governance mechanisms toward solutions amenable to more growth, profits, and control for big business.

Look at the 2016 Carbon Offsetting and Reduction Scheme for International Aviation, an agreement between the United Nation's International Civil Aviation Organization (ICAO) and the international aviation industry to pursue "carbon-neutral growth" after 2020. The ICAO President called the scheme a "bold decision and an historic moment." Britain's minister of aviation hailed it as an "unprecedented deal." Industry was equally enthusiastic. The deal is "at the cutting edge of efforts to combat climate change," declared the head of the International Airline Industry Association. It has "decoupled growth in aviation from growth in emissions," said a spokesperson for Britain's Air Transport Association.[17]

The airline industry has good reason for its enthusiasm for the direction of climate governance. Carbon pollution from aviation, which now comprises two to three percent of the global total, is on track to rise two to four times by 2050. Yet the airline industry is exempt from the 2015 Paris Agreement on climate change. Nor does the Carbon Offsetting and Reduction Scheme cover all airlines, excluding, for instance, those in Russia, India, and Brazil. Moreover, the scheme does not require any airline to actually cut greenhouse gas pollution. The airlines did agree to strive for greater technological efficiency. Yet the primary way they plan to attain carbon-neutral growth is by charging passengers an extra fee to offset emissions. The scheme does not explain the procedures for offsetting these emissions; nor does it say where or how this will occur, although presumably it will involve planting lots and lots of trees, somewhere. What is clear, however, is the scheme will allow the international aviation industry to fly more aircraft, burn more jet fuel, and spew more greenhouse gases into the atmosphere.[18]

Most governments have been more than happy to delegate the responsibility and authority for sustainability to the private sector, seeing this as a more efficient, less confrontational path forward. Market-oriented, bottom-up, nonbinding, and industry-friendly interventions – such as public–private partnerships and voluntary offsetting

– increasingly characterize global environmental governance. So do industry-guided and influenced certification schemes, such as the Forest Stewardship Council, the Marine Stewardship Council, the Roundtable on Sustainable Palm Oil, and the Round Table on Responsible Soy. And so do solutions that assume the necessity of moving forward with TNC investment, international trade, and industrial-scale production.

And shaping and controlling sustainability solutions is only part of the strategic value for big business of taking responsibility for sustainability. For agricultural, mining, and timber companies, for instance, it is dampening criticism by shifting culpability away from TNCs and onto the so-called "unsustainable" practices of smallholders, corrupt governments, illegal operators, and companies outside of their supply chains.

As we will see in the next chapter, taking responsibility for sustainability also serves three further purposes for big business. It is distracting from the continuing efforts by big business to avoid other responsibilities, such as paying reasonable wages, access fees, and taxes. It is concealing ongoing efforts by big business to thwart environmental regulations and hide exploitation deep in the shadows of supply chains. And it is functioning as a smokescreen to conceal poor, risky, and even illegal practices, as big business continues to pursue its core maxim: extract, exploit, expand.

4

The Dark Side of Big Business

Trust in big business is rising as the business of CSR deepens. Politicians are asking corporate executives to help negotiate international environmental agreements. Bureaucrats are welcoming their advice on how best to implement environmental legislation. Nonprofits are bringing them onto their advisory boards. And consumers are looking to them for reassurance of the safety and sustainability of products.

Trust in the value of corporate self-regulation, voluntary supply-chain auditing, and private certification is rising, too, even in the face of corporate scandals, and even as the environmental crisis continues to escalate. Corporations are "critical agents of positive change on a range of environment and civil rights issues," the executive director of the US Sierra Club, Michael Brune, told an audience of NGO and business leaders in 2017.[1]

Nonprofit leaders have also become increasingly trusting of the raw power of big business, seeing this power as a solution rather than a problem. "If you can get a company like Walmart right, it has a massive ripple effect," argues Peter Seligmann, CEO of Conservation International.[2]

Government leaders are similarly putting their trust in big business to lead sustainability. This would seem to be particularly true in the United States, especially among Republicans who advocate for deregulation and privatization. But even leading Democrats are turning to big business for sustainability leadership. "Critics seem to think that when we ask our businesses to innovate and reduce pollution and lead, they can't or they won't do it," then President Barack Obama said in a speech at Georgetown University. "But in America, we know that's not true." Former US Secretary of State John Kerry went even further when reflecting on the importance of the Paris Agreement on Climate Change going into force in 2016. "It is not going to be governments alone, or even principally, that solve the climate challenge. The private sector is the most important player."[3]

Does big business really deserve so much trust? Looking behind the scenes at the consequences of the competition for market shares, profits, and power suggests that policymakers and activists should be far more wary of the sustainability promises and aspirational goals of big business. The same TNCs promising to be sustainable and responsible are suppressing evidence of environmental damage, denying climate change, and funding anti-environmental think tanks. They are spilling oil, polluting waterways, and generating mountains of plastic and electronic waste. They are introducing new chemicals with little understanding of the consequences for the health of ecosystems and people. They are sourcing through long, complex supply chains that hide environmental consequences, cast ecological shadows worldwide, and minimize labor costs and on-the-ground responsibilities. And they are setting up shell companies, evading taxes, and buying off politicians.

In short, as we will see in this chapter, the same TNCs emblazoned in CSR are seeking out every possible competitive advantage, even if this means breaking the law now and then. Let us begin by looking at the ways TNCs avoid – and illegally evade – corporate taxes, thereby weakening the administrative capacity of states to protect ecosystems, and leaving many of them selling off even more natural resources to sustain basic services.

Evading taxes

If the profits are big enough, every TNC will push legal limits and risk their reputations. This helps explain why CSR has done so little to stop corporate tax avoidance. Around the world TNCs continue to shift and hide profits inside murky corporate structures. They continue to lobby governments for tax breaks, threatening to withdraw financing when political leaders push back. And they continue to finance political parties and pay off corrupt dictators to secure preferential deals.

Even companies with high brand trust are doing everything possible to avoid paying taxes. This is especially true in developing countries, where corporate tax avoidance is costing governments hundreds of billions of dollars a year: losses that help explain much of the poverty, inadequate social services, and weak environmental enforcement across the developing world.[4]

But corporate tax avoidance is common as well in jurisdictions with good governance. Over the past decade companies such as Amazon, Apple, Microsoft, Facebook, Google, and Starbucks have all butted heads with tax authorities across the European Union. The tactics of Google are typical. For years Google has been transferring its European profits to Bermuda, a tax haven, through Google Ireland Holdings, a company registered in Ireland where corporate tax rates and rules are highly favorable.

Google claims this is all perfectly legal. Whistleblowers came forward in 2013, however, alleging that Google's set-up was circumventing UK tax laws and claiming that Google Ireland was little more than an administrative office to avoid taxes. Margaret Hodge, chair of a British parliamentary committee looking into the allegations, was less than impressed with Google's legal justification of its tax structure, describing it as "devious, calculated and . . . unethical." This inquiry did little to alter Google's practices. In 2014 Google transferred around US$13 billion of its foreign earnings to Bermuda, paying roughly US$3 million in taxes on this income (a tax rate of about 0.024 percent). Nor has the controversy around Google's tax maneuvers seemed to hurt the company's global image or reputation as a CSR leader. According to the annual CSR survey by the Reputation Institute, consumers ranked Google as the world's "most responsible" in 2014, 2015, and again in 2016.[5]

Like Google, Apple also routes profits through Ireland. And, again just like Google, the company insists it is completely legal, even though the company's tax rate in Ireland was a mere 0.005 percent in 2014.[6] Tellingly, the European Commission ruled in 2016 that Ireland's tax deal with Apple from 1991 to 2015 was illegal under EU rules, and ordered the company to pay US$14.5 billion in back taxes and interest to Ireland (and possibly other states, if they were to pursue claims).

Apple's CEO, Tim Cook, was livid, calling the ruling "total political crap," and saying he would immediately appeal the decision.[7] Significantly, the ruling did not affect Apple's share price, once again signalling to big business the low risks and high gains of doing everything possible to avoid paying taxes. Plus, as investment analysts were quick to point out, with over US$230 billion in cash and securities on hand at the time, if absolutely necessary, Apple would have no trouble paying off these back taxes.

Starbucks in the UK has also gone to great lengths to avoid paying corporate taxes. The company launched in the UK in 1998. For years it faced public and governmental pressure to scrap its complex accounting and profit-shifting practices that left it consistently declaring losses and paying very little corporate tax; in 2015 the European Commission ruled that the tax break Starbucks was gaining in the Netherlands was illegal. Bending somewhat, that year Starbucks did end up paying corporate tax of £8.1 million to the UK government – but, revealingly, this tax bill was not far off the combined amount paid to the UK over the previous fourteen years (£8.6 million).[8]

Tax avoidance is just one of many enduring big business strategies to enhance profits and secure competitive advantages. To gain market dominance, companies are constantly pushing the legal limits of antitrust laws, as we saw in 2017 when the European Commission fined Google US$2.7 billion for anti-competitive practices for configuring its search engine to prioritize its shopping service. We even see some long-trusted brands, such as Volkswagen, brazenly breaking environmental laws to gain market access and sales advantages.

Breaking the law

Volkswagen's 2016 Annual Report – subtitled a "New Beginning" – says the company is now "committed to sustainable, transparent and responsible corporate governance."[9]

Volkswagen's new beginning included pleading guilty in 2017 to charges in the USA of conspiracy, fraud, and obstruction of justice for secretly installing illegal computer software into its diesel automobiles. Known as a "defeat device," this software kicked in during emissions testing to lower nitrogen oxide levels. Starting in 2009 this device put Volkswagen and Audi models on American roads that were spewing out pollution as much as forty times above the US legal limits.

It may seem commendable to take responsibility and plead guilty to criminal charges. Yet, when US investigators first became suspicious of what Volkswagen might be up to, the initial response of executives was to attack the investigation as incompetent and the science underlying the suspicions as faulty. One investigator would later tell the *New York Times*: "They tried to poke holes in our study and its methods, saying we didn't know what we were doing. They were very aggressive." Then, as incontrovertible proof of wrongdoing began to emerge in 2015, Volkswagen executives stalled, lied, and ordered employees to delete computer files and destroy evidence.[10]

Volkswagen's obfuscation didn't end there. Just weeks before pleading guilty to the US charges, the managing director of Volkswagen UK, Paul Willis, was telling members of the British parliament that the company had "misled nobody." When incredulous MPs pushed back, Willis ducked their questions, declaring himself "open" and, although unable to remember much, doing his best to answer "transparently." Conservative MP Mark Menzies was unimpressed. "You come before us and your mouth opens and words cascade out and then the next time you come before us those words have changed in meaning."[11]

The story of the defeat device is a reminder of the lengths even highly respected companies will go to expand markets and seek profits. Martin Winterkorn, the CEO of Volkswagen during the scandal, had set his sights on passing Toyota to become the world's biggest automaker. At the opening of a new Volkswagen plant in Tennessee in 2011 he confidently told a group of American lawmakers, "By 2018, we want to take our group to the very top of the global car industry."[12]

To take down Toyota, Winterkorn felt he needed a larger share of the American market. But his engineers were struggling to meet relatively high US emission standards without sacrificing the fuel efficiency and performance advantages of Volkswagen's diesel cars, which Winterkorn saw as having the best prospects of strong sales.

In retrospect, the solution – to compete against the Prius Hybrid by introducing into the American market "clean diesel" cars equipped with an emission-control disabling device to increase gas mileage – might look extraordinarily risky. Yet in many ways it is not that surprising given the competitive pressures on automakers and the large performance bonuses for CEOs. Volkswagen is not the first automaker to install a device to thwart environmental regulations. Others, including Volkswagen, installed technologies in the early 1970s to shut off pollution controls to enhance performance. And Volkswagen is unlikely to be the last. A company pleading guilty to criminal charges is definitely unusual; but, it is fair to say, trying to get around regulations is commonplace.

Volkswagen's defeat device suggests another lesson for those thinking through the potential for corporate self-regulation to advance global sustainability. In 2015, the year the scandal broke, Volkswagen reported losses of US$1.5 billion as revenues fell by twelve percent. By the time Volkswagen was pleading guilty in 2017, the company had already agreed to pay the American government US$4.3 billion in fines, and in the USA alone was looking at tens of billions of dollars in further costs to recall and repair the nearly 600,000 diesel cars sold with defeat devices (worldwide, as mentioned in the opening chapter, Volkswagen put the device in eleven million cars).

Yet here's the rub. In 2015, even with the fines,

bad publicity, and a decline in sales, Volkswagen was still the world's seventh biggest company by revenue turnover, up from eighth place the year before. And Volkswagen's sales resurged in 2016, with Audi sales in China leading the way. Around the world customers looking for a deal from a scandal-ridden company also helped offset some of the decline in Volkswagen's diesel sales in Europe and North America. That year, for the first time ever Volkswagen reached number one in new vehicle sales (with 10.3 million), knocking Toyota (10.2 million) out of first place – a spot Toyota had held since 2011 when the Tōhoku earthquake and tsunami disrupted industrial production across Japan, allowing General Motors to outsell them. In the end Winterkorn's prediction that Volkswagen would overtake Toyota by 2018 came true, two years ahead of schedule.

Winterkorn was forced to resign as CEO in 2015, retiring with the parting words, "I am not aware of any wrongdoing on my part."[13] A few Volkswagen employees have also faced criminal charges in the United States. Yet, when all is said and done, the scandal did not cost the company much. This outcome is surely not a good sign for those hoping CSR commitments and environmental self-regulation can hold corporate profit and growth compulsions at bay.

Volkswagen is far from the only big business to

survive – and then thrive – after a scandal. And it is far from the only one to fight back with lawyers, or sacrifice a few employees, or turn to Orwellian doublespeak to declare a new beginning. Look at the Swiss company Nestlé, the world's biggest food and beverage company. Notorious for contributing to a global health crisis in the 1970s by convincing mothers in developing countries to substitute infant formula for breast-milk, today Nestlé is claiming it is helping "billions of people" while striving "for zero environmental impact."[14]

Or consider BP. Since pleading guilty to criminal charges and agreeing to pay billions of dollars in fines and compensation for spilling oil into the Gulf of Mexico in 2010, BP has put its sustainability unit into overdrive. Bob Dudley, who became the CEO of BP following the 2010 spill, is head cheerleader for the unit, telling the world in 2017 (without irony, I should say) that the company's renewed environmental "strategy builds on two decades of action and advocacy on climate change."[15]

Obfuscation and obstruction

Of course, what the CEO of BP means by "action" could include lobbying against climate regulation and sabotaging climate science. For climate change, big oil as a whole has worked long and hard to generate scientific uncertainty, stall investigations, and send governmental inquiries into tailspins, all the while declaring a commitment to serving society.

The Exxon Mobil Corporation is a good example. Rex W. Tillerson – who after eleven years as CEO stepped down in 2017 to become US Secretary of State – wrote in his prefacing letter to ExxonMobil's 2015 *Corporate Citizenship Report*: "We have and will continue to engage relevant stakeholders to further develop climate science and broaden its understanding by society at large."[16]

Yet over the last half-century ExxonMobil has suppressed evidence of climate change, funded climate-change deniers, and obstructed regulatory action. Back in the 1970s in-house researchers for Exxon were already linking the burning of fossil fuels with a potential warming of the earth, a decade before the global community was starting to worry seriously about the possibility of climate change. "The most likely manner in which mankind is influencing the global climate is through carbon dioxide release from the burning of fossil fuels," a company scientist told Exxon executives in 1977.[17]

Keeping this research quiet, by the 1980s ExxonMobil had switched to attack mode, seeing climate science as a threat to its core business. It paid for advertising and opinion writing to question the accuracy of climate knowledge. It backed anti-environmental think tanks. And it financed counter-research to raise the levels of "uncertainty" for climate data and modeling.

By 2015 the story of ExxonMobil's early research and decades-long cover-up was leaking into the public realm. Writing in the *Guardian* that year, the bestselling author Bill McKibben reproached ExxonMobil for helping to "organize the most consequential lie in human history," his fury spilling over in his closing sentence: "In its greed Exxon helped – more than any other institution – to kill our planet."[18]

In 2016 US prosecutors launched fraud proceedings against the Exxon Mobil Corporation for concealing the risks of climate change (and thus exaggerating its oil assets to shareholders). During one of the trials in 2017 the attorney general of New York wrote to the court: "Exxon's top executives, and in particular, Mr. Tillerson, have made multiple representations that are . . . potentially false or misleading statements to investors and the public." The attorney general also revealed that from 2008 to 2015 Tillerson used an alias account – under the name "Wayne Tracker" (Tillerson's middle name is

Wayne) – to email back-and-forth when discussing climate change with his executives.[19]

Big oil's obstruction of environmentalism has been particularly strong. At times it even turns violent, as we saw when the Nigerian government executed Ken Saro-Wiwa (and eight others) in 1995 for protesting against Royal Dutch Shell's human rights and environmental record in the Niger Delta. Eleven years later Shell would settle a claim by descendants and victims that it had conspired with the government, paying out US$15.5 million, but admitting no wrongdoing. The money is no more than a "humanitarian gesture . . . a compassionate payment," the company said in a press release.[20]

TNC violence has been especially high in some sectors, such as industrial mining and logging in Africa, Latin America, and the Asia-Pacific. In places like the Philippines and Peru repression of indigenous peoples and local communities frequently characterizes industrial mining operations, including for the world's biggest mining company, Glencore. Yet, although some companies are definitely worse than others, it is also the case that obfuscation and obstruction of environmentalism have long been the modus operandi of big business as a whole. It is not always so obvious, however, especially for companies able to hide their activities in the shadows of complex corporate structures and long supply chains.

In the shadows

Understandably, TNCs with billion-dollar brands have always tried to avoid being accused of doublespeak or brazen illegal acts; furthermore, as we saw in Chapter 3, many are now positioning themselves as sustainability leaders to decrease the risk of becoming a target of a government investigation or civil society campaign. Over the past decade consumer-facing brands like Apple, Disney, and Starbucks have tried in particular to limit their exposure to poor supplier practices.

One approach has been to start buying more products certified as sustainable, responsible, and conflict-free. And to varying degrees certification is helping to improve sourcing practices, as we saw in Chapter 3 with timber certified by the Forest Stewardship Council, seafood certified by the Marine Stewardship Council, and palm oil certified by the Roundtable on Sustainable Palm Oil.

Yet industry eco-labels are often little more than advertising stickers to entice environmentally conscious consumers. And even third-party certification tends to produce mixed environmental benefits. These schemes frequently end up deflecting problems into new locations as suppliers who are unable (or unwilling) to meet certification requirements seek new buyers. Certification schemes can also create a false dichotomy between "sustainable" and "unsustainable" products, as we can now see happening with palm oil, soy, and beef. Such a dichotomy can create incentives to bribe officials and forge paperwork to gain certification. It can also empower a misleading discourse of "sustainable" companies buying "sustainable" products – with "others" (often smallholders and local firms) the real problem.

To further limit exposure to poor supplier practices, consumer-facing brands have also put in place reporting and auditing programs, essential for any meaningful compliance with codes of conduct or CSR standards. As with certification, these programs are doing far less to improve environmental and social management than the brands are telling consumers, NGOs, and governments.

Confidential supply-chain reporting is designed to support the business goals of brand buyers, while reporting for public disclosure tends to present the brand in the best possible light. The conclusion of a study of sustainability reporting in the Asia-Pacific is true around the world: "Due to the absence of mandatory standards, corporations handpick those metrics that they can easily measure and disclose information on these metrics while ignoring those that cannot be measured or those that could possibly show a darker side of the corporation in terms of their sustainability initiatives." Moreover, as another study of the history of sustainability reporting found, TNCs also tend to equate "narrow," "incomplete," and "partial reporting" with "actually *being sustainable*, or more commonly, with claims to be *moving towards sustainability*."[21]

Equally troubling, audits frequently fail to detect problems or violations, even in cases where a disaster later strikes (e.g., a chemical spill or factory fire). At the same time brands tend to only cut a firm out of its supply chain for a grievous misdeed – such as decorating McDonald's Happy Meal toys with leaded paint – or when doing so is valuable for placating social activists or reassuring consumers, such as when the toy company Mattel severed ties with Asia Pulp & Paper in 2011 following a campaign to shame Mattel for boxing its Barbie dolls in cardboard containing wood fiber from old-growth rainforests of Indonesia. Moreover, a supplier ejected from a supply chain may quickly find a new buyer, perhaps one with even lower standards.

For brand companies with a hundred thousand suppliers, at best auditors are only able to spot-check a handful each year. In addition, private auditors have less power than government auditors to investigate factories (e.g., look inside drawers and lockers) and protect whistleblowers, with private auditors in countries like China facing especially great obstacles. As one German executive noted, in China "I am prohibited from going to see parts of companies even though they are supplying to me and I am a major buyer." Additionally, some brands clearly do not want auditors to look too closely, alerting floor managers ahead of time to help the supplier pass an audit. "There is a whole industry of ethical auditors out there now who will find nothing if you pay them to go and find nothing," explains one labor rights advocate.[22]

Auditing tends as well to focus on a brand's Tier I suppliers, ignoring the ecological costs and labor exploitation in the labyrinth of Tier II and III suppliers. As one brand retailer said when discussing how this works for fair trade coffee, "I'm going to audit the crap out of your co-op coffee bean company to make sure you're actually paying the farmers. Who checks to see if the farmer is paying the pickers? Nobody!" The difficulty and expense of auditing large numbers of small businesses and family operations partly explains why brand companies avoid auditing below the first layer of suppliers. But some of the gaps and loopholes in the auditing of corporate codes and private certification schemes are intentional, as these help keep prices low for so-called ethical and sustainable supplies bought from Tier I firms. "We will audit as far down as the brand wants to go," explains one auditor.[23]

In short, audits are designed to protect the brand, not workers or the environment. When considering the value and effectiveness of audits, we need to keep in mind who is hiring the auditors, and whose interests audits serve. And we need to keep reminding ourselves why companies like Apple and Walmart and Nike are assuming the responsibility for the auditing of supply chains: it is enhancing their power to extract profits out of the shadows of a global economy of unsustainable consumption.

5

The Consumption Problem

More consumption means more sales and more profits. This grows economies, which creates jobs and prosperity. How could this be a problem? Besides, more consumption is necessary to feed, clothe, and house a fast-rising world population. Right?

The consequences of consumption, however, are far more complicated and multifaceted than this common narrative suggests. Much of today's global consumption is excessive and wasteful, with the degree of excess highly unequal across cultures and individuals. Consumption by the rich has been rising steadily over the past half-century, casting increasingly intense shadows of harm onto distant lands and future generations as food, natural resources, and waste zigzag through the world economy. Meanwhile, billions of people do not have adequate nutrition, potable water, or shelter, with degraded rural areas depopulating and urban slums growing increasingly crowded.

Corporate sustainability rarely ever reduces excessive, wasteful, or unequal consumption. Nor does it do much to lighten the shadows of consumption – and at times even makes things worse. On occasion, a CEO of big business may mention a need for less consumption, but always with a wink. "Our primary goal is to reduce our consumption," Walt Disney CEO Bob Iger said when explaining his company's sustainability strategy, "but we don't feel guilty about growing as a company."[1]

Three reasons stand out for the failure of corporate sustainability to make any real progress toward resolving the problem of consumption. First, as advertising and sales division spur consumption of all sorts, the CSR and sustainability units tend to shrug off profligate consumption as an unavoidable byproduct of affluence. Second, big-box retailers and brand manufacturers are reinvesting the savings from corporate sustainability to spur even higher levels of consumption globally, which in turn drives demand for the cheap energy and natural resources of transnational oil and mining companies. Third, the turn toward voluntary business standards and market mechanisms to offset ecological harms is doing relatively little to mitigate the global environmental consequences of rising rates of consumption.

Manufacturing overconsumption

For these reasons, big business is making the growing problem of overconsumption worse, not better. Overconsumption, most simply, is consumption that exceeds the capacity of ecosystems to regenerate, retain dynamic stability, and support future life. Telltale signs of overconsumption include the irreversible decline of renewable resources (such as fish, timber, water, and arable land), the exhaustion of nonrenewable resources (such as oil, gold, diamonds, phosphate, and coltan), the loss of entire ecosystems (such as grasslands, watersheds, and salt marshes), and the polluting of natural systems with carbon, e-waste, chemicals, and plastic.

Overconsumption for individuals occurs when they exceed their "fair earth share" – an amount each person could in theory consume without irreparably degrading the earth for future generations.[2] Overconsumption can also be measured at national, regional, and global scales. Ecological footprint analysis by the Global Footprint Network, for instance, estimates that if everyone on the earth were to consume like North Americans do today, we would need three to five Earths to regenerate natural systems and absorb the waste.

Overconsumption at the global scale is rising in part because more individuals are consuming more of everything. But it also connects closely with ostentatious and wasteful consumption, such as living in a 40-room mansion, driving a Hummer, or constantly upgrading products. Unequal wealth and consumer desires, however, only partly explain increasing rates of overconsumption.

In a process some call "commodification" and others "commoditization," since at least the beginning of the Industrial Revolution in the eighteenth century more and more of daily life has been turned into market transactions for ideas, services, and objects, with animals and people traded as products, and with advertisers equating the buying of "goods" with feelings of self-worth, pleasure, and happiness. At the same time governments have subsidized infrastructure (e.g., highways) and steered economies toward overconsumption, while international organizations – such as the World Bank, the International Monetary Fund, and the World Trade Organization – have provided financing and supported trading arrangements to increase the consumption of natural resources and industrial agricultural products.

The Consumption Problem

Commodification and globalization have reinforced the power of big business to manufacture excessive, unequal, and wasteful consumption. As we have seen, the vast majority of consumer-facing TNCs are now claiming a total commitment to sustainability, responsibility, and citizenship, emphasizing the generosity of their philanthropy and the environmental value of their programs to promote recycling, energy efficiency, less waste, and more conservation. Yet even a quick glance at their communication with shareholders and investors reveals a bullheaded focus on accelerating growth, building new factories and stores, enticing new customers, and generating higher profits – in other words, a total commitment to increasing consumption in any form.

Strategies to expand and remake consumption vary across TNCs. Ones like Apple and General Electric focus on branding, mass marketing, and upgrading. Ones like McDonald's and 7-Eleven concentrate on franchising. Ones like Walmart and Amazon emphasize discount sales and bulk purchases. Ones like Cartier and Tiffany sell luxury goods as status symbols. And ones like Louis Vuitton and Gucci push the newest season of designs. Yet in every case the underlying goal is the same: to get more people to buy more things.

The Consumption Problem

There are countless examples of big business manufacturing overconsumption. Consider the marketing of big, heavy SUVs. These vehicles are now, in the language of industry analysts, "the largest drivers of growth across all automobile markets, accounting for around twenty-nine percent of global sales in 2016. Over the past decade total auto sales have been rising especially quickly in emerging markets such as China and India. But, even with small car sales falling, total auto sales have also been increasing in mature markets like the United States as automakers push up sales of SUVs and pickup trucks with clever advertising, easy financing, and cash rebates. For the seventh straight year, total US auto sales set yet another record high in 2016, with Ford's F-Series pickup truck leading the charge. That year SUV and pickup sales accounted for sixty-three percent of total US auto sales, up from fifty percent in 2013.[3]

The history of sugar offers another example of how big business manufactures overconsumption. Over the course of the twentieth century average sugar consumption quadrupled, with caloric intake rising from an average of about 150 calories per day in the early 1960s to over 200 today. Americans consume the most sugar: on average over 126 grams a day, more than the British (93 grams) and

Canadians (89 grams), far more than the Italians (58 grams) and Japanese (57 grams), and way more than the Israelis (14.5 grams) and Indians (5 grams).[4]

In 2016 global sugar consumption yet again set a new record high, having climbed to over 170 million metric tons (up from 155 million metric tons in 2010). Sugar sweetens much of what we eat. It is in candy, cereal, cakes, and cookies. It is in jam, yogurt, and canned sauces. And it is in bread, soups and alcohol. One of the biggest uses, however, is for soft drinks, and the world's single biggest buyer of sugar is Coca-Cola.[5]

In recent years Coca-Cola has been shifting away slightly from using sugar to make its Coke, Fanta, Sprite, and sports beverages as people drink more of its diet and sugar-free products. At the same time Coca-Cola is quick to emphasize in its sustainability reports that it is now trying to use more of what it calls "sustainable" sugar: for instance, buying over one million metric tons in 2016 (mostly Bonsucro-certified sugar).

Yet even a cursory glance at the company's other reports shows its core business remains getting more people to buy more of its five hundred brands. Here, the vision is not of a healthy, sustainable world, but one where Coca-Cola controls an even larger share of the global soda market and where on average every person drinks at least 135–155 liters of soda a year, as is now the case in Argentina, the United States, Chile, and Mexico.

Already in 1980 the Coca-Cola Company, with sales of US$5.9 billion, was capturing more than thirty-five percent of the global soft drink market. In 2016 sales exceeded US$44 billion, with people drinking on average 1.9 billion servings a day of Coca-Cola brands. That year alone Coca-Cola introduced over five hundred new products to markets across the world – or, as the company proudly told its shareholders at year's end, "nearly two products launched per day."[6]

Coca-Cola is an exceptionally powerful company. But, of course, it is just one of many forces engineering taste preferences toward sweetness. Mars, Mondeléz, and Nestlé play leading roles. So do Hershey, Cadbury, Nestlé, and Ferrero, among many other companies. And there are many factors beyond sugar causing global rates of diabetes and obesity to rise, including the dietary impact of fast food, processed food, and meat companies. Yet there is no question that the dogged marketing of soft drinks by companies like Coca-Cola is a major reason why Americans consume so much sugar, why global consumption of sugar is now so high – and is still rising – and why the World Health Organization reports a more than doubling of obesity across the world from 1980 to 2014.

Tales of corporate re-engineering of consumer cultures could go on and on. We could look at Chiquita and the mass marketing of Cavendish bananas. Or at McDonald's, Burger King, and Wendy's and the consumption of fifty billion hamburgers a year in the USA alone. Or at De Beers and every culture's seemingly insatiable love for diamonds. Or at Procter & Gamble's campaign to turn China into a leading disposable diaper market by advertising Pampers as offering babies a longer and deeper sleep, making for smarter and healthier children. Going into more detail, however, is unnecessary as in every case a similar pattern emerges: big business, both legally and illegally, does everything in its power to sell more of its products.

One consequence is that corporate innovation has rarely ever reduced global consumption of anything. This holds true even when rapid technological progress takes holds, as a 2017 study in the journal *Technological Forecasting & Social Change* shows. One example is the miniaturization of silicon semiconductors. Compared to the 1970s it now takes far less material to produce one transistor. Yet global consumption of silicon has climbed steadily as companies make more products with silicon and as more people buy more products with silicon, from computers to smartphones to tablets.

The study in *Technological Forecasting & Social Change* did find a couple of examples of an absolute decline in consumption. This occurred when governments took strong action to end production, as with thallium, mercury, and asbestos. And this occurred when companies substituted new inputs to feed broader demand, as with the decline in wool consumption as the clothing industry turned to synthetic materials (or, as we will see in the next chapter, what may now be occurring with coal as producers switch to less-polluting energy sources). But, generally, gains from higher technological efficiency of corporations have almost always rebounded to stimulate even more consumption.[7]

Certainly, big business is not solely responsible for rising overconsumption. That would be an absurd claim. Yet given the dominance of the world's largest companies within the world economy (see Chapter 2 for details), big business is clearly the single biggest cause. This point deserves heavy underlining as so many governments and NGOs are now misguidedly looking to corporate self-regulation and eco-consumerism to govern us out of the global environmental crisis. A deeper look into the ecological shadows of consumption reveals the potential for catastrophe if we do not tackle this growing problem of overconsumption.

The shadows of consumption

The globalization of the world economy since World War II has been increasingly shifting the costs of rising overconsumption into ecosystems far from the eyes of the majority of consumers, degrading the Amazon, depleting the high seas, eroding Africa, and polluting the Arctic. These shadows of consumption include what economists often call "externalities," which arise when market prices do not reflect the full costs of production, such as emitting greenhouse gases. Shadow effects include as well, however, the intentional distancing of production costs and waste by states and firms; for instance, as they ship garbage and e-waste overseas or as they relocate dirty industries into poor, racialized neighborhoods. Deescalating our global environmental crisis will require confronting these hidden costs of overconsumption, especially by the wealthiest ten percent of the world's population, who now account, for example, for around half of the emissions of carbon dioxide arising from individual consumption.[8]

The Consumption Problem

The proliferation of chemical and electronic waste is one sign of the intensifying shadows of over-consumption. There are now more than 144,000 chemicals in commercial use, and for most of them we have very little understanding of the long term consequences as substances interact with each other and as they bioaccumulate in nature. And far more chemical pollution is on the way. Every year, for example, brings another forty-five to fifty million metric tons of e-waste as consumers discard cell-phones, computers, televisions, dishwashers, and microwaves: of this waste, only six to eight million metric tons is safely recycled, while much of the rest lands in the poorest regions of Asia and Africa.

The Arctic is now one of the planet's most con-taminated regions as persistent organic pollutants – such as dioxin, dichlorodiphenyltrichloroethane (DDT), and polychlorinated biphenyls (PCBs) – bounce across the earth like grasshoppers until settling in the coldest regions as the process of evaporation and precipitation comes to an end. Even the deepest recesses of the earth are filling with chemicals. Recent tests on crustaceans living in the inky blackness of the Mariana Trench, an eleven-kilometer deep crevice in the western Pacific Ocean, found exceptionally high levels of PCBs and polybrominated diphenyl ethers (PBDEs, a flame retardant in products like couches, pillows, and TVs). PCB levels in the crustaceans from the Mariana Trench were as much as fifty times higher than for crabs from the dirtiest waters of mainland China.[9]

The shadows of consumption on the earth's climate are equally alarming. Carbon dioxide, methane, and nitrous oxide emissions are the main technical causes of climate change, with carbon pollution accounting for around three-quarters of human-induced warming over the past century. The majority of this carbon pollution links to just 90 fossil fuel and cement companies, and big oil companies clearly have much to answer for.[10] But rising overconsumption is also a fundamental reason for rising greenhouse gases. Coal, oil, and natural gas fuels the making and recycling of consumer products. Construction, roadwork, and landfills are also major sources of greenhouse gases. So is the heating and cooling of homes and office towers. And so is the driving of cars, SUVs, and trucks, which, for instance, account for around one-fifth of US emissions.

Industrial food production is another major source of greenhouse gases. Land clearing emits carbon dioxide; rice cultivation, manure, and flatulating livestock spew methane; and organic and chemical fertilizers release nitrous oxide. The shipping, trucking, and flying of food across vast distances is also a significant source of emissions. In total, the global agricultural system accounts for around one-quarter of anthropogenic greenhouse gases.[11]

The earth's climate is drifting into an ever-deeper crisis as the shadows of mass production, transportation, and industrial agriculture continue to intensify. Already, average temperatures have gone up by more than 1°C since pre-industrial times. And far more warming is likely. In pre-industrial times the amount of carbon dioxide in the atmosphere was 270 to 275 parts per million of molecules; today, the figure is over 400 ppm and rising. Methane, with more than twenty-five times the long-term warming power of carbon, is also increasing. The ten years before 2017 was the hottest decade ever recorded; and 2016 was the hottest year so far. If trends continue, average temperatures could well rise 3 to 4°C above pre-industrial times by the end of this century; if trends worsen, we could even see a rise as high as 6°C.

Climate change, moreover, is just one of many interacting and reinforcing environmental changes brought on by the shadows of overconsumption. Fresh water is growing scarcer for the world's poorest people as industry, industrial agriculture, and well-off individuals consume ever more; billions of people do not even have enough fresh water to meet basic needs. Meanwhile, global rates of extraction, degradation, pollution, and ecosystem collapse are continuing to rise. Biodiversity loss is one critical sign. Every day, of the eight to nine million species, between ten and five hundred are becoming extinct, with rising numbers of species under threat as rates of loss accelerate.[12]

Especially telling is the consequences of the shadows of consumption for tropical rainforests. More than half of these forests have been cleared since 1950, and of those remaining only fifteen percent are still intact enough to retain full biodiversity. For many decades now deforestation of the tropics has been one of the biggest causes of climate change, accounting for around fifteen percent of global anthropogenic carbon pollution. Yet still, every year, even in the face of an escalating global biodiversity crisis, millions of hectares of old-growth tropical forests are logged and then razed for palm oil estates, soy plantations, and cattle ranching.

Ocean life is suffering, too, in the shadows of humanity's rising consumption. Since 1950 the number of seabirds has fallen by more than seventy percent, overhunted, poisoned by human waste, tangled in fishing gear, and killed off by oil spills and climate change.[13] One-fifth of coral reefs have been destroyed, and at least half of the remaining reefs are under threat from global warming, acidification, chemical contamination, fishing, and tourism. The populations of more than half of commercial fish species have fallen by more than ninety percent since the beginning of industrial fishing. Some, such as the cod off the east coast of North America, have crashed to less than one percent of their original population. These declines have done little to slow commercial harvests. Each year at least half-a-trillion fish are consumed or discarded as bycatch, an amount which, if lined up, would touch the sun.[14]

The plastic crisis

The growing crisis of plastic waste vividly illustrates the destructive power of the ecological shadows of overconsumption. Plastic production has gone up sixfold since the 1970s, and is now around 330 million metric tons a year – roughly equal to the weight of all the people on the planet, assuming an average weight of 43–45 kilograms per person. And production of plastic is set to double again over the next twenty to thirty years.

Around forty percent of global plastic production goes into packaging, and the vast majority of plastic packaging is thrown away after a single use. Every year companies are now producing around five hundred billion plastic bottles, an increase of two hundred billion since 2004. Rising consumption of plastic bottles of water and soda explains much of this increase. Coca-Cola alone is now selling 108 to 128 billion plastic bottles, according to calculations done by Greenpeace in 2017. On our present trajectory, within the next five years companies will be selling around six hundred billion plastic bottles a year.[15]

Plastic garbage is now swirling in immense eddies in the Pacific, Atlantic, and Indian oceans. The Arctic has become one of the most polluted regions for plastic, with bottle caps and fishing gear littering island shorelines, and with over a trillion microplastics (less than five millimeters in diameter) trapped in the sea ice. Trying to explain what is going on in the Arctic, in 2017 the scientist Wouter Jan Strietman described the seas around Svalbard – an archipelago halfway between Norway and the North Pole – as "the drain hole of the Gulf Stream."[16]

On a recent trip to the Svalbard islands Strietman and his colleagues found the shores littered with plastic, with bottle caps accounting for eight percent of the identifiable plastic pieces. Yet this plastic comprises a tiny fraction of global ocean pollution. Trillions of pieces of plastic – or roughly two hundred million metric tons – are now in the oceans. And another five to thirteen million metric tons of plastic are flowing in annually. If the trends over the past decade continue, the Ellen MacArthur Foundation calculates that by the middle of this century the oceans could contain more plastic than fish (by total weight).[17]

Henderson Island, never inhabited, and lying in the middle of the South Pacific Ocean between New Zealand and Chile, offers a rare glimpse into the shadows of plastic consumption. Both New Zealand and Chile are more than 5,500 kilometers away from the tiny coral atoll, which is just thirty-seven square kilometers in size. The UN Educational, Scientific and Cultural Organization (UNESCO) lists Henderson Island as a world heritage site, noting that it is "one of the few atolls in the world whose ecology has been practically untouched by a human presence" – "the ideal context for studying the dynamics of insular evolution and natural selection."[18]

Yet here, Australian and British researchers recently found thirty-eight million pieces of plastic washed ashore, making the remote island one of the world's most densely polluted ever discovered. Hermit crabs are now housing themselves in the plastic remains, including one seen scurrying along carrying an Avon cosmetics jar.

And the plastic debris keeps coming. Each day, as the researchers toiled away, another thirteen thousand pieces of plastic washed onto the sandy beaches of Henderson Island. "This plastic is old, it's brittle, it's sharp, it's toxic," said lead researcher Jennifer Lavers of the University of Tasmania. "It was really quite tragic seeing these gorgeous crabs scuttling about, living in our waste."[19]

Defining our age

It would seem we are now well into a new geo-logic epoch: the age of *Homo sapiens*, or what many people are now calling the Anthropocene, with humans causing earth-scale changes akin to an asteroid hitting the earth. Already, we have warmed our climate, cleared more than half of the tropical forests, driven innumerable species into extinction, emptied the oceans of much of its life, and polluted every nook and cranny of the planet. Relying on overconsumption to propel economic growth and business prosperity is without question

an ecological mistake. And voluntary corporate sustainability, eco-markets, and eco-consumerism are
obviously doing very little to address the problem
of overconsumption.

Given the arc of history since World War II, far
more environmental degradation would seem to be
on the way. Yet I don't see total destruction ahead.
And, as I argue in my concluding chapter, there are
definitely opportunities to lessen the extent of the
coming destruction.

6

Less Destruction

Surveying the escalating environmental crisis, and thinking about our personal role as the consumers of the products of big business, can feel depressing, even gut-wrenching, as it was for me when learning of the waves of plastic now crashing onto the shores of Henderson Island. Still, returning to this book's anchoring question, I do not think big business is going to destroy our planet: not completely, anyway. Let us review why I have come to this conclusion.

First of all, despite the extraordinary power of big business over the world economy, global rules, and political narratives, and even though this power is rising in all its forms, big business is still only one of many interacting forces degrading the earth. The myopia of governments, the actions of small business, and the desires of billions of people are major factors. Modern cycles of degradation also arise out of centuries of ecological imperialism and economic exploitation. For sure, big business is a powerful force of destruction. Nevertheless, I think it is fair to conclude that the evils of world politics – nuclear warfare, biological terrorism, militarism – are far more likely to obliterate us.

There are, however, other good (and more optimistic) reasons to think big business won't destroy our planet. Significantly, as ecological and economic turbulence intensifies, business self-preservation will help prevent total destruction. Already, large numbers of TNCs are exploiting the increasing scarcity of natural resources and the growing instability of the global environment to gain competitive advantages and expand markets, including eco-markets. This is definitely improving management on some measures. As we saw in Chapter 3, for example, as the competition for natural resources intensifies, the efficiency of production is rising; and as the competition for eco-consumers builds, the energy efficiency of many household products, such as dishwashers, refrigerators, and washing machines, is increasing.

Big business is improving environmental performance in other ways, too. TNCs are redesigning products to save on transportation costs. They are making plastic bottle caps smaller and lighter. They are selling three-ply toilet paper and concentrated laundry detergent. And they are miniaturizing electronics.

Most redesigns aim to capture new markets or reduce per unit costs of shipping goods across the world's oceans, skies, and highways. But sometimes, as sustainability managers are always eager to point out, these "new and improved" products are also reducing per unit waste and pollution emissions. At the same time TNCs are recycling more metal, glass, paper, and plastic to generate a reliable resource stream for further production. And they are installing rooftop solar panels to diversify energy sources as global warming generates uncertainty in coal, oil, and natural gas markets.

The intensifying competition for resources is further encouraging big business to do more to control global supply chains. Over the past decade, as Chapter 3 reviewed, TNCs have set up codes of conduct, environmental reporting requirements, auditing systems, certification standards, and recycling and waste management programs for their supply chains. Partly, TNCs are trying to protect brand value and better manage reputational risks. But gaining more control over supply chains is also offering many competitive advantages.

It is helping TNCs to track and buy the highest quality and least expensive inputs, from coltan to cocoa to coffee. It is helping them cut production costs, increase profit margins, and slash prices to increase sales and open up markets. And it is allowing them to claim sustainability leadership by reducing waste, improving efficiencies, and lowering the per unit greenhouse gas emissions of relatively low-performing suppliers.

Granted, as the previous chapter showed, these are fairly modest gains in comparison with the scale and force of the escalating global environmental crisis. Moreover, as we have seen, the compulsive pursuit by big business of ever-more power, profits, and growth is overriding many of these gains. Yet I also put some hope in the power of the global environmental movement – including a gradual strengthening of environmental regulations and international norms since the 1960s – to prevent big business from completely destroying our planet.

The power of environmentalism

Environmental management has clearly been improving since the 1960s, at least in some places, for some people, in some time periods. Very few states, for instance, still legally allow the hunting of whales, the trading of endangered species, or the dumping of toxic sludge into local rivers. The international community of states has also managed to solve a few planetary-scale environmental crises. One of the best examples is the coming together of states after 1987 to work with DuPont and other chemical companies to phase out chlorofluorocarbons (CFCs), which were destroying the ozone layer after drifting skyward from our refrigerators, air conditioners, and home insulation. As a result of these efforts, the ozone layer, necessary for life on earth, is now set to regenerate over the next fifty years.

There are many other examples of environmental improvements. Thousands of certification and offsetting programs are now offering more environmentally friendly options for consumers, and most cultures have shifted somewhat toward more environmentally conscious consumption, from organic coffee to eco-tourism. Worldwide, more than 200,000 parklands, nature reserves, and ocean sanctuaries have been put in place, and today more than one-seventh of the earth's landmass is officially "protected" by governments.[1] Before 2006, Australia's Great Barrier Reef was the only marine protected area larger than 200,000 square kilometers; yet over the decade since 2006 governments announced another eighteen massive marine parks, covering more than thirteen million square kilometers of ocean.[2]

On land, meanwhile, state and community rangers in Africa are fining and jailing poachers in the fight to save elephants, rhinos, and hippos. Parts of Africa have also been reforested. The Green Belt Movement alone, a community organization set up by Nobel laureate Wangari Maathai in Kenya in 1977, has planted more than fifty million trees across Africa.

The influence of environmentalism is clear across many other areas, too. In terms of per unit of economic output, over the past few decades technological advances in resource extraction, manufacturing, and transportation have been steadily improving energy efficiency, reducing pollution, and eliminating unnecessary waste. Buildings are meeting higher water, waste, energy, and emission standards. Highways are more durable and road construction does more to account for habitat disruption. The incineration of garbage and the recycling of e-waste are following stricter environmental guidelines, especially in developed countries. And pollution has decreased markedly in well-off cities, such as in London, where smog during one particularly bad week in late 1952 contributed to the premature deaths of as many as twelve thousand residents.[3]

The production of solar and wind energy has also been surging over the past decade, with China at the forefront. Worldwide, solar, wind, and renewable power grew yet again in 2016, up fourteen percent. Led by China, installed global solar capacity went up fifty percent that year, although it is important to note that solar energy still only accounts for a small portion of world electricity production.

Significantly, though, as renewable power increases we're now starting to see a decline in coal consumption. In China, coal consumption fell in 2014, in 2015, and again in 2016. Worldwide consumption of coal also fell in 2015 and again in 2016 as businesses and governments switched to natural gas and renewable energy. The UK led the way following mine closures and the introduction of a carbon tax, with coal consumption in 2016 dropping by more than fifty percent, hitting levels not seen since the 1800s.[4]

In some ways the corporate embrace of sustainability as a marketing and management tool is also creating opportunities for environmental activists to influence corporate production, retailing, and marketing. We saw this, for instance, in the campaign to shame global brands into no longer sourcing palm oil linked to tropical deforestation. Starting in 2008 when Greenpeace convinced Unilever's Dove soap to switch to buying palm oil certified as sustainable, activists then went after scores of other brands, from Nestlé's Kit Kat chocolate bar to Procter & Gamble's Head & Shoulders shampoo to PepsiCo's Doritos tortilla chips. By 2016 just about every global brand had made a public commitment to "zero deforestation" and was promising to only source palm oil from the Roundtable on Sustainable Palm Oil (sales of RSPO-certified palm oil rose five-fold from 2010 to 2016).

The influence of environmental NGOs and grass-roots movements only goes so far, however; and for many activists the politics of opposing business remains cutthroat, especially in developing countries. Those benefiting the most from destroying our planet continue to control the main levers of power – from armies to bureaucracies to corporations to the media – and environmentalists are routinely jailed and murdered.

At least 185 environmental activists lost their lives in 2015, forty-two of whom were opposing industrial mining. Others died fighting against illegal logging, agricultural plantations, hydroelectric dams, and poaching, with Brazil, the Philippines,

Colombia, Peru, and Nicaragua leading the death tally. "As demand for products like minerals, timber and palm oil continues, governments, companies and criminal gangs are seizing land in defiance of the people who live on it," explains Billy Kyte, who documented the murders of activists in 2015 for the NGO Global Witness. "Communities that take a stand are increasingly finding themselves in the firing line of companies' private security, state forces and a thriving market for contract killers." Even more environmental and land activists were murdered in 2016: at least two hundred.[5]

The failures of environmentalism

Our planetary crisis would surely be worse without the global spread of environmentalism and the courage of grassroots activists like those in Brazil, the Philippines, and Colombia. Yet the net results are not adding up to anything close to planetary sustainability as the power of big business continues to grow, as inequality continues to rise, and as the ecological shadows of overconsumption continue to intensify. If anything, as this book underlines, since the mid-2000s corporate, state, and to a lesser extent NGO environmentalism have been doing less and less to challenge the societal, political, and corporate forces and narratives driving unequal, wasteful, and excessive consumption, with environmentalists increasingly looking instead to eco-consumerism as a way to protect the global environment.

Today, just about every mainstream sustainability policy reflects the demands of economic growth, the interests of transnational corporations, and the concerns of wealthy individuals – reflecting a growing dominance of what I think of as the "environmentalism of the rich."[6] The vast majority of international and national environmental initiatives are failing to reduce unsustainable consumption or slow rates of degradation on a global scale. Moreover, the costs and benefits of environmental solutions are highly uneven, with rich and powerful individuals and places almost always faring better than marginalized peoples and vulnerable ecosystems.

Remarkably often, when governments and firms are claiming to be solving a problem they are in fact deflecting the problem into another jurisdiction or into the future, casting ecological and social shadows that make the global situation worse, not better. This was the case in the 1970s and 1980s, for instance, when the United States phased out leaded gasoline at home, while American TNCs increased leaded gasoline exports to Africa. This was the case as well after China banned logging in its natural forests in 1998, only to become in short order the world's biggest importer of tropical and boreal wood, much of it illegally logged and smuggled into the country.

The world's richest people are now consuming five, ten, even fifty times more than their fair earth share. Meanwhile, consumption of increasingly scarce natural resources continue to grow, while lands and oceans continue to fill with consumer waste. Yet global environmental governance largely ignores the growing inequality of consumption and the extremes of wealth creation.

States see more consumption, of any kind, as economic growth, prosperity, and a sign of effective governance. Corporations see more consumption as sales, profits, and a sign of a strong market. Even most NGOs do not portray consumption as a problem, although there are some exceptions, such as Adbusters, a counterculture magazine and activist network calling for less consumption and greater social justice.

Significantly, as we have seen in this book, since the mid-2000s the world's biggest TNCs have been steadily gaining power over global environmental governance as they increasingly claim to be sustainability leaders. States have reacted by backing market-based governance and delegating authority to corporations to self-regulate. Large numbers of NGOs have responded by cooperating and partnering with these TNCs.

But, as the previous chapter showed, corporate sustainability does little to reduce inequitable, conspicuous, or wasteful consumption, as at the end of the day corporations are seeking more sales, profits, and growth, not the social sustainability of communities or the ecological integrity of the earth. Eco-consumption, although able to ease the footprints of a few conscientious consumers, has little power to shift global patterns of consumption. At the same time corporate sustainability is primarily aiming to find savings to invest in more factories and stores, and to sell more products, regardless of need, durability, or net ecological costs.

Sustainability for big business is about wasting less to produce more, so, even though each unit of production may end up causing less environmental harm, overall harm frequently ends up rising. We see this pattern, for instance, with ongoing corporate strategies to manufacture and market nondurable, disposable, and quickly obsolescent products, not just at home, but all around the world. And we see this as corporations continue to engineer the overconsumption of unhealthy food and fast food.

The corporate understanding of sustainability does not see the tripling in sales of plastic water bottles as a problem, but as a logical outcome of strategically investing the savings from manufacturing, packaging, and transporting water bottles more efficiently. For this reason, although the environmental gains from corporate sustainability governance can look impressive when measuring, say, changes in the tonnage of recycled metal, glass, or plastic, the gains look far less impressive when evaluating the global environmental consequences of, say, the volume of plastic flowing into the ocean, or the amount of chemicals spilling into rivers and lakes.

These failures of corporate sustainability have done little to impede the growing power of TNCs within global environmental governance or the trend toward more moderate environmental discourses and demands from civil society. Since the mid-2000s large numbers of local, national, and international NGOs have joined forces with business, raising funds by cobranding products, and advocating for eco-technologies, eco-products, and eco-certification as solutions for global environmental problems. This more moderate stance is helping raise funds for conservation and community development. Yet praising big business as "sustainability partners" is also muting criticism of the ongoing role of these companies in manufacturing overconsumption.

At the same time states and corporations are capturing and manipulating the discourse of sustainability, and misinformation and exaggerations are rampant on all sides. There is also a dark side to TNCs now claiming to be responsible and sustainable. We saw this in Chapter 4 when looking at Volkswagen's scheme to install secret software to evade emission regulations. We saw it with ExxonMobil's clandestine strategy to back climate skepticism. And we saw it again with the tactics of Starbucks, Apple, and Google to avoid taxes.

In this context environmentalists who advocate for state policies of sustainable development, corporate responsibility, eco-markets, certification, and eco-consumption risk becoming little more than mouthpieces for corporate strategies to deflect criticism of the status quo, stall reforms, and legitimize a highly unequal, exploitative, and destructive global political economy of consumption. Such initiatives bring other risks too, aggravating unequal, wasteful, and excessive consumption, as well as deflecting attention from broader corporate and state efforts to drive overconsumption.

Corporate sustainability and global environmentalism, then, would seem to be doing enough to stop big business from destroying our planet completely, but not enough to prevent immense damage by the end of this century. States and societies clearly need to do far more to curb the power of big business to drive unsustainable production and consumption.

Doing less damage

Given our current trajectory, I don't see a way to avoid damaging a great deal more of the earth over the course of this century. But the extent of the coming damage is not set in stone. Can we avoid another one- to two-degree Celsius rise in global temperatures by 2100? Probably not, but we can certainly still avoid another three- to four-degree Celsius increase. Will the earth lose lots more forests, wetlands, and species? Again, this seems inescapable.

Can we avoid, however, a sixth mass extinction? Or significantly decrease plastic, air, and chemical pollution? Or do a much better job protecting the last of the rainforests, coral reefs, and biodiversity hotspots? Here, I think we can.

But any chance of this happening will require governments, nonprofits, and consumers to put far less faith in corporate self-reporting and self-regulation to solve global environmental problems. And it will necessitate far louder questioning of the motives and impacts of big business as well as much tougher state regulation of TNCs, including confronting the increasing power of big business to manufacture overconsumption.

Corporate sustainability, as we have seen time and again in this book, is helping on some measures. There's certainly value in encouraging big business to continue to increase recycling, improve building standards, and reduce packaging waste. In a few cases big business may even advocate for better environmental practices, as is now occurring in the USA for clean power as more than seventy percent of the top one hundred companies pursue renewable energy targets.[7] And to at least a limited extent NGOs willing to partner with big business – such as WWF, Conservation International, and the Environmental Defense Fund – are helping to conserve some environmental values.

But by its very nature corporate self-governance cannot deescalate the global environmental crisis. CSR philanthropy and corporate sustainability are first and foremost power levers and business tools. For any chance of moving toward global sustainability, governments and NGOs need to keep this in mind, working to take back, rather than surrender, power over global environmental governance.

Reining in TNCs will require multiscale and multilayered governance, as no single state, international organization, or activist network will ever be able to do this alone. Stronger incentives and regulations to enhance corporate disclosures and the accuracy of consumer information would help. So would more laws to increase the transparency of the global financial system, such as the 2010 US Dodd–Frank Wall Street Reform and Consumer Protection Act. There is also a need for more auditors and government inspectors with enough power to truly investigate big business practices.

It would further help to enhance the legal powers of governments and international organizations to hold corporations accountable for handling illicit products causing social conflict and environmental destruction. Countries of the European Union, for instance, have been trying to do this since 2013 with the EU Timber Regulation that requires companies to conduct "due diligence" to "make every effort to ensure that the wood they trade in is legal."[8]

Binding international agreements to constrain the tax, environmental, labor, and human rights practices of transnational firms would also go a long way toward reducing the damage of TNCs. One example would be a treaty like the one the UN Human Rights Council is now considering "to regulate, in international human rights law, the activities of transnational corporations and other business enterprises."[9]

More generally, governments could reduce the damage of big business by passing stronger environmental legislation with ambitious targets and timelines, moving faster and harder than industry will go voluntarily, pushing back when big business is recalcitrant. Here, it is vital to give indigenous peoples and local communities more say when granting extraction and production rights to TNCs. Imposing higher levels of precaution when approving new chemicals, technologies, and industrial processes would help, too. So would holding more producers liable for post-consumer waste – what some governments are calling "extended producer responsibility." Incentivizing manufacturers to reuse more of the material and energy from consumer waste streams would also help. And so would closing legal loopholes, reducing the influence of big business on all levels of politics, and enforcing the laws currently on the books.

But states alone will never be able to fully restrain the destructive compulsions of big business. We need community activists, investigative journalists, and NGOs like Global Witness and Greenpeace to continue to expose corporate crimes, from bribing politicians to deceiving regulators to smuggling blood diamonds. And we need environmental and consumer activists to keep fighting as politicians backed by big business maneuver to repeal regulations already in place, as happened in 2017 with the Dodd–Frank Act after President Donald Trump came to power and the Republicans gained control of Congress.

At the same time grassroots movements will need to continue to oppose development projects and industrial extraction that is destroying local environments, as happened in El Salvador leading up to the 2008 moratorium on large-scale metal mining and the subsequent 2017 formal ban (to protect the country's freshwater supply). Social media campaigns will need to keep challenging the narrative of consumer capitalism and keep reminding people of the consequences of wasteful and excessive consumption. Activists will need to continue to expose – and shame – brands for evading taxes, employing slave labor, and falsifying certification. And resistance campaigns like the Occupy movement will need to keep disrupting the rationalizations of elites who are getting rich by destroying the planet.

Going forward, governments and civil society organizations must be careful to not let the feel-good rhetoric of CSR and the incremental advances from corporate sustainability further weaken their resolve to dismantle corporate monopolies, oppose corporate mergers, and confront the growing inequality of wealth and consumption. We need states to prosecute TNCs for corruption, misconduct, and fraud, as attorneys are now trying to do in the USA with ExxonMobil. And we need them to prosecute corporate executives for participating in transnational environmental crimes, supporting organizations such as the International Criminal Court in The Hague, which in 2016 announced it would start treating "the destruction of the environment, the illegal exploitation of natural resources or the illegal dispossession of land" as crimes against humanity.[10]

Of course, such actions to rein in big business are going to face strong opposition. If anything, the next few decades are likely to see even bigger, more powerful transnational corporations with even more control over our planet's fate. Unless it is in their interest, TNCs will never simply roll over to the demands of social movements, governments, or communities. And they'll never stop contesting norms, discourses, and laws that challenge their capacity to extract profits, concentrate wealth, and gain power.

Nor is corporate sustainability ever going to lead

us to planetary sustainability. Yet, as this chapter shows, there are ways to push big business to go beyond corporate sustainability. And there are some hopeful signs this is beginning to occur.

All TNCs have an innate vulnerability: they need public trust, markets, and resources to thrive. Intriguingly, the strategy to brand themselves as responsible and sustainable has left TNCs more financially exposed to environmental criticism. While the power of big business over global governance is clearly rising, so is the power of social justice and environmental advocates to devalue brands by exposing their illegal, unethical, and unsustainable activities. This growing power to cut into the financial bottom line of TNCs may offer a way to push big business to do even less damage to the earth, as long as regulators, activists, and consumers can avoid being lulled into complacency by the money, first-class comforts, and modest gains on offer from voluntary corporate governance.

Further Reading

There is a vast and growing literature evaluating the consequences of business for global sustainability. To begin, you may want to widen my Chapter 1 snapshot of the global environmental crisis. There are many reasonable books to choose from, including Clive Hamilton, *Defiant Earth* (Polity, 2017) and Edward O. Wilson, *Half-Earth* (W.W. Norton, 2016). For those wanting a more historical understanding of the reasons for today's environmental crisis, one of the best options is John Robert McNeill and Peter Engelke, *The Great Acceleration* (Belknap Press, 2014). Also worth everyone's time is the new edition of Alfred W. Crosby's classic study of the devastating ecological consequences of imperialism, *Ecological Imperialism* (Cambridge University Press, 2004).

There is an extensive literature on the role of

corporations in escalating this crisis. Joel Bakan's book, *The Corporation* (Free Press, 2004), is an excellent entry point, as is his acclaimed documentary based on this book (http://thecorporation. com). Naomi Klein offers a more recent, and highly accessible, analysis of the consequences of rising corporate power for climate change in *This Changes Everything* (Simon & Schuster, 2014); the documentary of her book is also worth watching (https:// thefilm.thischangeseverything.org). Klein's earlier books – *No Logo* (Viking Canada, 2000) and *The Shock Doctrine* (Picador, 2007) – also offer many insights into the destructive nature of corporations. Christopher Wright and Daniel Nyberg provide a more scholarly take in *Climate Change, Capitalism, and Corporations* (Cambridge University Press, 2015). For those looking for analysis of these themes set deeply in the writings of Karl Marx and Marxist theorists, the best book of recent years is Jason W. Moore, *Capitalism in the Web of Life* (Verso Books, 2015).

All of the books above contain insights into Chapter 2's analysis of how and where the power of big business is rising. For further insights into the power of business in American politics, see Robert B. Reich, *Supercapitalism* (Alfred A. Knopf, 2007). David C. Korten's *When Corporations Rule the World*, 3rd edn. (Berrett-Koehler Publishers, 2015), which examines the growing concentration of wealth and power among the world's top companies (building on the first edition, published in 1997), is also worth reading. Another fine analysis of the rising power of TNCs is Susan George, *Shadow Sovereigns: How Global Corporations are Seizing Power* (Polity, 2015). The following books might also interest those curious to learn more about the rise of a "super-rich": Chrystia Freeland, *Plutocrats* (Doubleday Canada, 2012) and Iain Hay, ed., *Geographies of the Super-Rich* (Edward Elgar, 2013).

My book with Jane Lister, *Eco-Business* (MIT Press, 2013), is a logical entry point into the literature reviewed in Chapter 3 on how and why TNCs are using CSR and sustainability programs to compete for competitive advantages, including cost savings, market growth, production efficiencies, and brand value. For further analysis of how sustainability discourses and policies have come to serve business interests, see Adrian Parr, *Hijacking Sustainability* (MIT Press, 2012) and Adrian Parr, *The Wrath of Capital* (Columbia University Press, 2013). My book with Genevieve LeBaron – *Protest Inc.* (Polity, 2014) – adds an analysis of why, and to what extent, NGOs are embracing big-business sustainability, and how this is altering the agendas and discourse of activists. Lisa Ann Richey and Stefano Ponte's *Brand Aid* (University of Minnesota Press, 2011) further extends the understanding of the consequences of NGO–business partnerships for social activism.

CSR and business sustainability, as Chapter 3 shows, is improving corporate performance on some measures. There are many possible books to choose from to extend my analysis of where, when, and how gains are occurring. For a small sampling, see Geoffrey Jones, *Profits and Sustainability* (Oxford University Press, 2017); Andrew J. Hoffman, *Finding Purpose* (Greenleaf, 2016); Alfred A. Marcus, *Innovations in Sustainability* (Cambridge University Press, 2015); John Mackey and Raj Sisodia, *Conscious Capitalism* (Harvard Business Review Press, 2014); and William McDonough and Michael Braungart, *The Upcycle* (North Point, 2013).

Walmart, as Chapter 3 notes, led the corporate charge to seek business gains from pursuing aspects of environmental sustainability. For a popular account, see Edward Humes, *Force of Nature* (Harper-Collins, 2011). For an analysis of Walmart's role in advancing the uptake of conflict-free gold and ethical jewelry, see Michael J. Bloomfield, *Dirty*

Gold (MIT Press, 2017). For a history of Walmart more generally, see Nelson Lichtenstein, *The Retail Revolution* (Metropolitan Books, 2009).

There is an equally expansive literature on the destructive practices of firms claiming to be responsible, and how, as Chapter 4 surveys, CSR can act as a smokescreen to hide poor practices. One of the best books on how big business sabotages critical narratives is Naomi Oreskes and Erik M. Conway, *Merchants of Doubt* (Bloomsbury Press, 2010). Kerryn Higgs in her book *Collision Course* (MIT Press, 2014) provides a thorough history of the backlash against the idea of "limits to growth," which the "Club of Rome" popularized in the early 1970s. There are also many books investigating the dubious practices of specific firms, such as Bartow J. Elmore, *Citizen Coke* (W. W. Norton, 2015).

My books, *The Shadows of Consumption* (MIT Press, 2008) and *Environmentalism of the Rich* (MIT Press, 2016), would be reasonable starting points for digging further into Chapter 5's analysis of the role of big business in fostering excessive, unequal, and wasteful consumption. So too would Annie Leonard's *The Story of Stuff* (Free Press, 2010). For those wanting to delve deeper into the academic debates surrounding the environmental consequences of consumption, one of the best books taking a "consumption angle" is Thomas Princen, Michael Maniates, and Ken Conca, eds., *Confronting Consumption* (MIT Press, 2002).

For those interested in the consequences of advertising for children's consumption, a first-rate book is Joel Bakan, *Childhood Under Siege* (Simon & Schuster, 2011). Juliet B. Schor's bestselling *Born to Buy* (Scribner, 2004) also offers many insights into the culture of consumerism, as does: Tim Wu, *The Attention Merchants* (Alfred A. Knopf, 2016); Tim Jackson, *Prosperity without Growth*, 2nd edn. (Routledge, 2017); Nato Thompson, *Culture as Weapon* (Melville House Publishing, 2017); and Frank Trentmann, *Empire of Things* (Harper, 2017).

Polity's Resources series provides a wide-ranging source of books on the global politics of natural resource consumption, and includes my 2011 book *Timber* (with Jane Lister), as well as many others, such as Elizabeth R. DeSombre and J. Samuel Barkin, *Fish* (2011); Michael Nest, *Coltan* (2011); David Lewis Feldman, *Water* (2012); Derek Hall, *Land* (2013); Gavin Fridell, *Coffee* (2014); Ian Smillie, *Diamonds* (2014); Ben Richardson, *Sugar* (2015); Adam Sneyd, *Cotton* (2016); Jennifer Clapp, *Food*, 2nd edn. (2016); Bill Winders, *Grains* (2016); Gavin Bridge and Philippe Le Billon, *Oil*,

2nd edn. (2017); Anthony Burke, *Uranium* (2017); and Kristy Leissle, *Cocoa* (2018).

To fill out the sketch in Chapter 5 of the deteriorating state of the global environment, see Ian Angus, *Facing the Anthropocene* (NYU Press, 2016); George M. Woodwell, *A World to Live In* (MIT Press, 2016); Elizabeth Kolbert, *The Sixth Extinction* (Henry Holt and Company, 2014); Jared M. Diamond, *Collapse*, revised edn. (Penguin, 2011); and Bill McKibben, *Eaarth* (Times Books, 2010).

To expand on Chapter 6's conclusions on the failure of global environmental governance, it might help to begin with Thomas Hale, David Held, and Kevin Young, *Gridlock* (Polity, 2013), although you should then follow up with the more optimistic analysis in Thomas Hale and David Held, eds., *Beyond Gridlock* (Polity, 2017). Susan George's *Whose Crisis, Whose Future?* (Polity, 2010) also offers a lively critique of global governance.

For analyses of the prospects and limits of private environmental governance, see A. Claire Cutler and Thomas Dietz, eds., *The Politics of Private Transnational Governance by Contract* (Routledge, 2017). For a critique of certification as a governance instrument, see Scott Poynton, *Beyond Certification* (Greenleaf, 2015). For a sampling of analyses of private governance, see Jessica F. Green, *Rethinking Private Authority* (Princeton University Press, 2014); Graeme Auld, *Constructing Private Governance* (Yale University Press, 2014); and Jennifer Clapp and Doris Fuchs, eds., *Corporate Power in Global Agrifood Governance* (MIT Press, 2009).

There is also a large literature on what might comprise a global politics of sustainability, and how and why this politics must constrain the destructive impulses of big business. For a deeper understanding of what the majority of environmentalists would see as the principles of sustainability, see Randall Curren and Ellen Metzger, *Living Well Now and in the Future* (MIT Press, 2017); Leslie Paul Thiele, *Sustainability* (Polity, 2013); and Thomas Princen, *The Logic of Sufficiency* (MIT Press, 2005).

The pathways toward global sustainability are not going to be easy to find, and figuring out a politics to constrain big business will involve multiscale, complex governance. My book with Jennifer Clapp, *Paths to a Green World*, 2nd edn. (MIT Press, 2011) offers a typology to evaluate the strengths and weaknesses of the main approaches currently in play within global environmental politics. John Dryzek's book, *The Politics of the Earth*, 3rd edn. (Oxford University Press, 2013) also offers a helpful summary of the various discourses.

After reading these books, it would then make sense to dive into the literature on what might constitute effective global environmental governance, including the overview by Kate O'Neill, *The Environment and International Relations*, 2nd edn. (Cambridge University Press, 2017), as well as more specific analyses, such as Simon Nicholson and Sikina Jinnah, eds., *New Earth Politics* (MIT Press, 2016); Paul F. Steinberg, *Who Rules the Earth?* (Oxford University Press, 2015); and Frank Biermann, *Earth System Governance* (MIT Press, 2014).

Notes

1 Total Destruction?

1 Estimates of "deforestation" vary depending on the definition (e.g., from less than 30% of canopy cover to less than 10%) as well as the methodology for calculating loss, renewal, and integrity (e.g., using satellite imaging or country reporting). The estimate of annual tropical deforestation as high as ten million hectares is from the World Resources Institute (for 2014). My conversion to soccer fields assumes one soccer field is equal to 0.8 hectares (approximately the size of the fields under Federation Internationale de Football Association [FIFA] rules) (31,536,000 seconds in a year, so one hectare cleared every 3.15 seconds, or one soccer field every 2.52 seconds). The estimate of the percentage of primate species facing extinction is from Alejandro Estrada et al., "Impending Extinction Crisis of the World's Primates," *Sciences Advances* 3 (1) (2017): 1–16.

2 Polman is quoted in Jo Confino, "Rio+20," *Guardian*, June 21, 2012.
3 For details (and my quotes), see Nike (www.nike.com); Monsanto (www.monsantofund.org); Volkswagen, *Sustainability Report 2010*, p. 9.
4 Muhtar Kent, the CEO of Coca-Cola in 2010 (he stepped down in 2017), is quoted in Andrew L. Shapiro, "Coca-Cola Goes Green," *Forbes*, January 29, 2010; Pepsi's CEO, Indra Nooyi, is quoted in PepsiCo, "PepsiCo Launches 2025 Sustainability Agenda . . .," News Release, October 17, 2016 (www.pepsico.com).
5 Walmart, "Sustainability," (corporate.walmart.com).
6 Andrew J. Hoffman, "Businesses Need to Go . . .," *The Conversation*, December 11, 2016.
7 For analysis of the variable power of big business over environmental policy in the United States, as well as the varying capacity of environmental policies to restrain corporate actions, see Sheldon Kamieniecki, *Corporate America and Environmental Policy* (Stanford University Press, 2006); Michael E. Kraft and Sheldon Kamieniecki, eds., *Business and Environmental Policy* (MIT Press, 2007). For a study of the influence of German environmentalism, see Frank Uekötter, *The Greenest Nation?* (MIT Press, 2014). For an analysis of the power of environmental policy in the European Union, see Tom Delreux and Sander Happaerts, *Environmental Policy and Politics in the European Union* (Palgrave, 2016); for a comparative study of environmental regulation in Europe and the USA, see David Vogel, *The*

Politics of Precaution (Princeton University Press, 2012).

8 Ronie Garcia-Johnson, *Exporting Environmentalism* (MIT Press, 2000).

9 See, for example, Lydia Bals and Wendy Tate, eds., *Implementing Triple Bottom Line Sustainability into Global Supply Chains* (Greenleaf, 2016); David Chandler, *Strategic Corporate Social Responsibility*, 4th edn. (Sage, 2016); Andrew Crane and Dirk Matten, eds., *Business Ethics* (Oxford University Press, 2016).

10 Joel Bakan, *The Corporation* (Free Press, 2004).

11 Kern is quoted in "Amazon and Starbucks ..." *Guardian*, September 2, 2016.

12 Peter Dauvergne, *The Shadows of Consumption* (MIT Press, 2008).

13 Patagonia, *Environmental + Social Initiatives* (2016), http://www.patagonia.com.

2 *The Rising Power of Big Business*

1 Global Justice Now, *Controlling Corporations* (September 2016); Oxfam International, *An Economy for the 99%* (January, 2017). The Forbes list of billionaires is at www.forbes.com/billionaires.

2 Alfred W. Crosby, *Ecological Imperialism*, new edition (Cambridge University Press, 2004); William A. Pettigrew, *Freedom's Debt* (University of North Carolina Press, 2013); Philip Lawson, *The East India Company* (Routledge, 2013; first published in 1993).

3 T. Christian Miller and Jonathan Jones, "Firestone

and the Warlord," *ProPublica* (with PBS Frontline), November 18, 2014 (www.propublica.org).

4 Nelson Lichtenstein, *The Retail Revolution* (Metropolitan Books, 2009); Charles Fishman, *The Wal-Mart Effect* (Penguin, 2006); Anita Chan, ed., *Walmart in China* (Cornell University Press, 2011).

5 For data on the world's 500 biggest corporations, see Fortune Global 500 (fortune.com/global500); for America's biggest firms, see Fortune 500 (fortune.com/fortune500).

6 This estimate is from the Interpublic Group (IPG), a marketing firm (see www.interpublic.com).

7 See Colin K. Khoury et al., "Increasing Homogeneity in Global Food Supplies and the Implications for Food Security," *Proceedings of the National Academy of Sciences* 111 (11) (2014): 4001–4006; Rosamond L. Naylor, "Oil Crops, Aquaculture, and the Rising Role of Demand," *Global Food Security* 11 (2016): 17–25.

8 See Iain Hay, ed., *Geographies of the Super-Rich* (Edward Elgar, 2013); Chrystia Freeland, *Plutocrats* (Doubleday Canada, 2012). For analyses of the corporatization of activism, see Peter Dauvergne and Genevieve LeBaron, *Protest Inc.* (Polity, 2014); Lisa Ann Richey and Stefano Ponte, *Brand Aid* (University of Minnesota Press, 2011); for higher education, see Jamie Brownlee, *Academia, Inc.* (Fernwood Publishing, 2015).

9 Hillary Clinton, "Being Pro-Business . . .," *Quartz*, October 20, 2015. For the merger data, see Barry C. Lynn, "America's Monopolies . . .," *The Atlantic*, February 22, 2017.

10 David C. Korten, *When Corporations Rule the World*, 3rd edn. (Berrett-Koehler, 2015), p. 19. Also see Susan George, *Shadow Sovereigns: How Global Corporations are Seizing Power* (Polity, 2015).

11 Boehm is quoted in Ann Hui, "What Happens . . .," *The Globe and Mail*, September 16, 2016; Bebb is quoted in John Vidal, "Farming Mega-Mergers . . .," *Guardian*, September 26, 2016. Also see Jennifer Clapp and Doris Fuchs, eds., *Corporate Power in Global Agrifood Governance* (MIT Press, 2009).

12 Oleg V. Petrenko et al., "Corporate Social Responsibility or CEO Narcissism?" *Strategic Management Journal* 37 (2) (2016): 262–79.

13 Feike Sijbesma is quoted in Elisabeth Braw, "DSM's CEO," *Guardian*, October 25, 2013.

14 Polman is quoted in Jo Confino, "Unilever's Paul Polman," *Guardian*, April 24, 2012.

15 McDonald is quoted in Jo Confino, "Proctor & Gamble . . .," *Guardian*, September 26, 2012; Nooyi is quoted in Robert Safian, "How PepsiCo CEO . . .," *Fast Company* (www.fastcompany.com), January 9, 2017.

3 The Business of CSR

1 John Elkington deserves credit for igniting the conversation on the value of a triple bottom line. See John Elkington, "Towards the Sustainable Corporation," *California Management Review* 36 (2) (1994): 90–100. The definition of sustainable development is from World Commission on Environment

and Development, *Our Common Future* (Oxford University Press, 1987), p. 43.

2 Monsanto (www.monsanto.com); Monsanto Fund (www.monsantofund.org); ExxonMobil, *2016 Worldwide Giving Report*

3 BP's CEO is quoted in BP, *Sustainability Report 2016*, April 6, 2017, p. 1; Coca-Cola's CEO is quoted in Coca-Cola, *Sustainability Update 2015/16*, p. 3.

4 McDonald's Corporation, under the tab Sustainability (corporate.mcdonalds.com).

5 Peter Benson and Stuart Kirsch, "Corporate Oxymorons," *Dialectical Anthropology* 34 (1) (2010): 45–48.

6 Apple, *Apple Supplier Code of Conduct*, Version 4.1.1, effective date: January 1, 2015.

7 The Cola-Cola Britain figures are in Zlata Rodionova, "Coca-Cola Produces . . .," *Independent*, April 9, 2017. The MacArthur initiative, called the New Plastics Economy, is at https://newplasticseconomy. org.

8 Peter Dauvergne and Jane Lister, *Eco-Business* (MIT Press, 2013). For broader analyses, see Adrian Parr, *Hijacking Sustainability* (MIT Press, 2012); Adrian Parr, *The Wrath of Capital* (Columbia University Press, 2013).

9 For examples of research on how CSR and eco-business have unfolded differently across firms, see Michael J. Bloomfield, *Dirty Gold* (MIT Press, 2017); Elizabeth Chrun, Nives Dolšak, and Aseem Prakash, "Corporate Environmentalism," *Annual Review of Environment and Resources* 41 (2016):

341–362; Hamish van der Ven, "Socializing the C-Suite," *Business and Politics* 16 (1) (2014): 31–63. For literature on the commitment to sustainability of some CEOs and managers, see Geoffrey Jones, *Profits and Sustainability* (Oxford University Press, 2017); Andrew J. Hoffman, *Finding Purpose* (Greenleaf, 2016).

10 Edward Humes, *Force of Nature* (HarperCollins, 2011).

11 Walmart, *2016 Giving Report*, p. 2. For a critique of the hunger relief programs of big business, see Andrew Fisher, *Big Hunger* (MIT Press, 2017).

12 See Walmart, *2016 Global Responsibility Report*, 2016, pp. 70–9; Walmart, "Sustainability," at http://corporate.walmart.com.

13 Roberts and Krupp are quoted in Walmart, "Walmart Launches Project Gigaton . . .," Press Release, April 19, 2017.

14 Palt is quoted in Eillie Anzilotti, "How L'Oreal . . .," *Fast Company*, March 23, 2017.

15 Kent is quoted in Andrew L. Shapiro, "Coca-Cola Goes Green," *Forbes*, January 29, 2010.

16 Allison Marchildon, "Corporate Responsibility or Corporate Power?" *Journal of Political Power* 9 (1) (2016), p. 60.

17 The ICAO President is quoted in Oliver Milman, "First Deal . . .," *Guardian*, October 6, 2016; Britain's aviation minister and Air Transport Association spokesperson are quoted in Roger Harrabin, "Aviation Industry . . .," *BBC News*, October 7; the head of the International Airline Industry Association is quoted

in Kristine Owram, "Airlines Claim 'Paris Moment' . . .," *The Financial Post*, October 6, 2016.

18 ICAO, "Carbon Offsetting and Reduction Scheme for International Aviation (State Signatories as of October 12, 2016)," UN International Civil Aviation Organization, at www.icao.int.

4 *The Dark Side of Big Business*

1 Brune is quoted in Heather Clancy, "Why More NGOs . . .," *GreenBiz*, February 18, 2017.

2 Seligmann is quoted in Heather Clancy, "How Conservation International . . .," *GreenBiz*, May 18, 2015.

3 Obama's speech is reprinted in Tom Randall, "'We Need to Act'," *Bloomberg*, June 25, 2013; Kerry is quoted in Kelli Barrett, "Hundreds of US Companies . . .," *GreenBiz*, November 18, 2016.

4 Ernesto Crivelli, Ruud De Mooij, and Michael Keen, *Base Erosion, Profit Shifting and Developing Countries*, IMF Working Paper, WP/15/118, May 2015.

5 Hodge is quoted in Simon Bowers and Rajeev Syal, "MP on Google . . .," *Guardian*, May 16, 2013. See also Abigail Tracy, "Google Moved . . .," *Forbes*, February 19, 2016; the Reputation Institute (www.reputationinstitute.com).

6 Sean Farrell and Henry McDonald, "Apple Ordered . . .," *Guardian*, August 30, 2016.

7 Cook is quoted in "Amazon and Starbucks . . ." *Guardian*, September 2, 2016.

8 Katherine Campbell and Duane Helleloid, "Starbucks: Social Responsibility and Tax Avoidance," *Journal of Accounting Education* 37 (2016): 38–60; Rob Davies, "Starbucks Pays . . .," *Guardian*, December 15, 2015.

9 Volkswagen, *Annual Report 2016*.

10 The investigator is quoted in Danny Hakim, Aaron M. Kessler, and Jack Ewing, "As Volkswagen . . .," *New York Times*, September 26, 2015; see also "Volkswagen Pleads Guilty . . .," *Guardian*, March 10, 2017.

11 Willis' remarks are reprinted in "Volkswagen Boss Says . . .," *Guardian*, February 21, 2017.

12 Winterkorn is quoted in Hakim, Kessler, and Ewing (full cite above).

13 Winterkorn's parting remark is in Hakim, Kessler, and Ewing (full cite above). For details see Marco Frigessi di Rattalma, ed., *The Dieselgate* (Springer, 2017).

14 See Nestlé, "Nestlé in Society," www.nestle.com.

15 Bob Dudley, Introductory Letter (dated April 6, 2017), in BP, *Sustainability Report 2016*, p. 1.

16 Rex W. Tillerson, "Chairman's Letter," *Corporate Citizenship Report*, 2015.

17 The ExxonMobil scientist is quoted in Neela Banerjee, Lisa Song, and David Hasemyer, "Exxon," *InsideClimateNews*, September 16, 2015. Also see, Naomi Oreskes and Erik M. Conway, *Merchants of Doubt* (Bloomsbury Press, 2010); James Hoggan (with Richard Littlemore), *Climate Cover-Up* (Greystone Books, 2009).

18 Bill McKibben, "Exxon's Climate Lie," *Guardian*, October 14, 2015.

19 The NY attorney general's letter is quoted in Karen Freifeld, "Rex Tillerson . . .," *Time*, March 13, 2017.

20 Shell's press release is quoted in Hakeem O. Yusuf and Kamil Omoteso, "Combating Environmental Irresponsibility of Transnational Corporations in Africa," *Local Environment* 21 (11) (2016), p. 1378.

21 The first study is Kaushik Sridhar and Grant Jones, "The Three Fundamental Criticisms of the Triple Bottom Line Approach," *Asian Journal of Business Ethics* 2 (1) (2013), quote on p. 108; the second study is Markus J. Milne and Rob Gray, "W(h)ither Ecology?" *Journal of Business Ethics* 118 (1) (2013), quote on p. 24.

22 The German buyer and the labor activist are quoted in Genevieve LeBaron, Jane Lister, and Peter Dauvergne, "Governing Global Supply Chain Sustainability Through the Ethical Audit Regime," *Globalizations* 14 (6) (2017), pp. 970–1.

23 The brand retailer and the auditor are quoted in LeBaron, Lister, Dauvergne, "Governing," p. 968.

5 The Consumption Problem

1 Eric Wesoff, "Disney CEO . . .," *GreenTech Media*, March 4, 2010 (www.greentechmedia.com).

2 William E. Rees and Jennie Moore, "Ecological Footprints, Fair Earth-Shares and Urbanization," in Robert Vale and Brenda Vale, eds., *Living within a*

Fair Share Ecological Footprint (Routledge, 2013), p. 16.

3 The quote "the largest drivers" is from JATO, "Global Car Sales . . .," February 9, 2017 (www.jato.com). The US auto data are summarized in Associated Press, "2016 U.S. Auto Sales . . .," *Los Angeles Times*, January 4, 2017.

4 See Ben Richardson, *Sugar* (Polity, 2015), pp. 2, 24; Euromonitor, as summarized in Roberto A. Ferdman, "Where People . . .," *Washington Post*, February 5, 2015.

5 The data on sugar consumption are from US Department of Agriculture, *Sugar: World Markets and Trade*, May 2017; for a critique of Coca-Cola, see Bartow J. Elmore, *Citizen Coke* (W. W. Norton, 2015).

6 Coca-Cola Company, "2016 Year in Review," "Over 500 New Products," www.coca-colacompany.com.

7 Christopher L. Magee and Tessaleno C. Devezas, "A Simple Extension of Dematerialization Theory," *Technological Forecasting & Social Change* 117 (April 2017): 196–205.

8 Oxfam, "Extreme Carbon Inequality," Briefing, December 2, 2015.

9 Alan J. Jamieson et al., "Bioaccumulation of Persistent Organic Pollutants in the Deepest Ocean Fauna," *Nature Ecology & Evolution* 1 (2017): DOI: 10.1038/s41559-016-0051.

10 Richard Heede, "Tracing Anthropogenic Carbon Dioxide and Methane Emissions to Fossil Fuel and

Cement Producers, 1854–2010," *Climatic Change* 122 (1) (2014): 229–41.

11 Eskild H. Bennetzen, Pete Smith, and John R. Porter, "Agricultural Production and Greenhouse Gas Emissions from World Regions," *Global Environmental Change* 37 (March 2016): 43–55.

12 Richard Monastersky, "Biodiversity," *Nature* 516 (7530), December 11, 2014: 159–61; Gerardo Ceballos et al., "Accelerated Modern Human–Induced Species Losses," *Science Advances* 1 (5), June 19, 2015.

13 Michelle Paleczny et al., "Population Trend of the World's Monitored Seabirds, 1950–2010," *PLOS ONE*, June 9, 2015.

14 Jonathan Balcombe, *What a Fish Knows* (Straus and Giroux, 2016).

15 Sandra Laville and Matthew Taylor, "A Million Bottles . . .," *Guardian*, June 28, 2017.

16 Rachel W. Obbarde et al., "Global Warming Releases Microplastic Legacy Frozen in Arctic Sea Ice," *Earth's Future* 2 (6) (2014): 315–20; Strietman is quoted in Damien Carrington, "Plastic Polluted Arctic Islands . . .," *Guardian*, June 16, 2017.

17 Marcus Eriksen et al., "Plastic Pollution in the World's Oceans," *PLOS ONE* 9 (12) (2014); Jenna R. Jambeck et al., "Plastic Waste Inputs from Land into the Ocean," *Science* 347 (6223), February 13, 2015: 768–71; the estimate of more plastic than fish by 2050 is from the Ellen MacArthur Foundation, *New Plastics Economy* (2017), p. 16.

18 UNESCO, "World Heritage List: Henderson Island" (http://whc.unesco.org/en/list/487).

19 Lavers is quoted in Elle Hunt, "38 Million Pieces . . .," *Guardian*, May 15, 2017. See also Jennifer L. Lavers and Alexander L. Bond, "Exceptional and Rapid Accumulation of Anthropogenic Debris on One of the World's Most Remote and Pristine Islands," *Proceedings of the National Academy of Sciences* 114 (23) (2017): 6052-5.

6 Less Destruction

1 Marine Deguignet et al., *2014 United Nations List of Protected Areas* (UN Environment Programme, 2014), p. 1.

2 Justin Alger and Peter Dauvergne, "The Politics of Pacific Ocean Conservation," *Pacific Affairs* 90 (1) (2017): 29–50.

3 Michelle L. Bell, Devra L. Davis, and Tony Fletcher, "A Retrospective Assessment of Mortality from the London Smog Episode of 1952," *Environmental Health Perspectives* 112 (1) (2004), p. 8.

4 The coal consumption data are from BP, summarized in Adam Vaughan, "Global Demand . . .," *Guardian*, June 13, 2017; Adam Vaughan, "Solar Power . . .," *Guardian*, March 7, 2017. For an analysis of environmental politics in China, see Judith Shapiro, *China's Environmental Challenges*, 2nd edn. (Polity, 2016).

5 Kyte is quoted in Oliver Holmes, "Environmental Activist . . .," *Guardian*, June 20, 2016. For details,

see Global Witness, *On Dangerous Ground* (2016); Global Witness, *Defenders of the Earth* (2017).

6 See Peter Dauvergne, *Environmentalism of the Rich* (MIT Press, 2016).

7 Advanced Energy Economy, *2016 Corporate Advanced Energy Commitments* (2016).

8 European Commission, "New EU Timber Regulation Comes into Effect in the European Union," Press Release, 2013.

9 United Nations, *Report of the Human Rights Council*, General Assembly Official Records, 69th Session, Supplement No. 53 (A/69/53) (2014), p. 157.

10 International Criminal Court, Office of the Prosecutor, *Policy Paper on Case Selection and Prioritisation*, September 15, 2016, p. 14.